Preaching the Word of God

REV. FR. ANTHONY CONIARIS

Preaching the Word of God

HOLY CROSS
ORTHODOX PRESS

Rev. Fr. Anthony Coniaris

PREACHING THE WORD OF GOD

© Copyright 1983 Holy Cross Orthodox Press
Second Edition, January 2018

Line drawing, p. 8, by Predrag Ilievski, © Newrome Press

Library of Congress Cataloging in Publication Data

Coniaris, Anthony M.
    Preaching the Word of God.

(The Saint John Chrysostom lectures on preaching)
1. Preaching—Addresses, essays, lectures.I.Title.
II. Series
BV422.C66 1983   251   8318416
ISBN 9780916586652

Holy Cross Orthodox Press
50 Goddard Avenue
Brookline, Massachusetts, 02445
Tel. 617-850-1321
Email: press@hchc.edu

Contents

Preface

The Saint John Chrysostom Lectures on Preaching are given annually at the Holy Cross Greek Orthodox School of Theology/Hellenic College, Brookline Massachusetts, and are sponsored by the members of St. Mary's Greek Orthodox Church, Minneapolis, Minnesota, whom we would like to thank very much for their generosity.

The Saint John Chrysostom Lectures on Preaching allow Holy Cross Greek Orthodox School of Theology to invite outstanding scholar-preachers to share their faith, learning, and experience with the students and faculty of Holy Cross and Hellenic College, thus providing an opportunity for spiritual enrichment and deepening of faith in God's living word.

Father Anthony Coniaris, a priest of the Greek Orthodox Church, an outstanding preacher of deep faith, and a prolific author, was invited to give the third annual Saint Chrysostom Lectures on Preaching. In place of the three lectures given at Holy Cross, Father Coniaris generously offered Holy Cross Press an entire volume entitled: Preaching The Word Of God. Although directed primarily to those who preach or wish to preach the word of God, the present volume offers much more in terms of spiritual nourishment to all Christians. It is in fact a book that can be read with great profit by everyone interested in a living faith. To Father Anthony, then, we owe many thanks not only for the present volume but also for suggesting the idea of sponsoring the Saint Chrysostom Lectures on Preaching to the members of his parish. To him and to them our deep appreciation on behalf of Holy Cross/Hellenic College and Holy Cross Orthodox Press.

N. Michael Vaporis
Dean, Hellenic College

I
The Priority of Preaching

The priority of preaching was established by Jesus himself when he commanded his disciples, "Go therefore and make disciples of all nations...teaching them to observe all that I have commanded you; and, lo, I am with you always, to the close of the age" (Mt 28.19-20). When Simon Peter confessed his love for Jesus, the Master replied, "Feed my lambs" (Jn 21.15).

Saint Paul established the priority of preaching more than once in his epistles. He says he was called by God "to make the word of God fully known, the mystery hidden for ages and generations but now made manifest to the saints. To them God chose to make known how great among the Gentiles are the riches of the glory of this mystery, which is Christ in you, the hope of glory. Him we proclaim...that we may present every man mature in Christ. For this I toil, striving with all the energy which he mightily inspires in me" (Col 1.25-29). Few persons have spoken more strongly of the priority of preaching than Saint Paul, especially in 1 Corinthians 9.16, "For if I preach the gospel, that gives me no ground for boasting. For necessity is laid upon me. Woe to me if I do not preach the gospel!" "So we are ambassadors for Christ," he says in 2 Corinthians 5.20, "God making his appeal through us." In preaching, God literally communicates his word through us. In Romans he writes, "So faith comes from what is heard, and what is heard comes by the preaching of Christ" (Rom 10.17) and "How beautiful are the feet of those who preach the good news" (Rom 10.15). If faith is to be born, we need to hear the word of God preached by someone who is sent by God. The very sacraments themselves cannot exist without preaching, since there is no sacrament without faith and no faith without preaching. Ephraim the Syrian goes so far as to say that "He [Jesus] entered the womb [of Mary] through her ear" at the Annunciation.

The priority of preaching is evident in the writings of the early Church Fathers. Much of their theology was written originally in the form of homilies and commentaries on the various books of the Bible. Theology itself was born of homiletical preaching.

It is inspiring to see the priority of preaching lived out in contemporary times in the Soviet Union in the ministry of Father Dimitrii Dudko.

When asked to discontinue his preaching, he replied, "Why did Christ say, 'Go and preach? People are saved by preaching. Should I then be afraid? If they throw me in jail, I'll preach even there. Preaching is my main job... Preaching is the priest's first obligation, and without it I can't conceive what my ministry would be like."[1] It is no wonder that Saint Gregory called preaching "the first duty of all."

---

[1]   Dimitri Dudko, *Our Hope* (Crestwood, N.Y., 1977).

The Liturgy itself testifies to the priority of preaching. For the preaching of the word is not tacked on at the end of the Liturgy, but comes right in the middle of it. The proper place for the sermon is following the reading of the gospel lesson. In fact, the first part of the Liturgy is called the Liturgy of the Catechumens or the Liturgy of the Word, since it consists in the reading of the epistle and gospel and their explanation in the sermon. The entire first part of the Liturgy is dedicated to the preaching of the gospel to the unbelievers and the preparation of the catechumens for baptism. According to the Church Fathers, there are two communions in the Liturgy. We commune first with Christ as the word of God (Liturgy of the Word), and then with Christ as the bread of life (Liturgy of the Faithful). In both communions we partake of Christ. First we break the word of God, then we break the bread of life. The preaching of the gospel (Mt 28.19) and the Eucharist are wedded together inseparably in the Liturgies of the Orthodox Church.

We do injustice to the priority of preaching when we make it appear as though it is not part and parcel of the Liturgy. We do this by tacking the sermon on at the conclusion of the Liturgy, or by omitting it completely during the summer months, or whenever we need to shorten the service. The sermon is not optional; it is an essential part of the Liturgy. It is a real communion with Jesus. As we would never think of omitting the second communion (the Eucharist) from the Liturgy, so we should never omit the first communion (the word of God).

Members of the Orthodox Consultation on "Preaching and Teaching the Christian Faith Today" which met in Yugoslavia in 1980 stated:

> The priest must never separate the *kerygma* of Christ, i.e., the teaching, proclamation and exhortation of the Scripture from the Liturgy; this *kerygma* is part of the very fabric of the Liturgy. There is an analogy of this link between the teaching and the sacrifice (*anaphora*) and the eating (*koinonia*) to be seen in the life of our Lord when he first taught the people and then offered himself in his body and blood on behalf of all.[2]

I must share with you at this point the words of Metropolitan Constantine of Pringiponessos:

> It is not enough, therefore, simply to perform liturgical rites and suppose that the spiritual and sacramental needs of the faithful are adequately met. In each of its aspects, Liturgy is an expression—indeed, a revelation—of the redemptive word of God within the Church and for the life of the world. That word is celebrated repeatedly in the Holy Eucharist and in the other sacraments. But that word must also be preached. Within the context of the Church's sacramental celebration, the word must be proclaimed with faithfulness, with power and in contemporary idiom in order to guide the faithful into an ever fuller understanding and receptivity of God's saving work on their behalf. The heart of that proclamation is a summons to repentance and to faith. It is a call, a vo-

---

[2]   "Orthodox Consultation on Preaching and Teaching the Christian Faith Today" *St. Valdimir's Theological Quarterly*, 25 (1981).

cation based not upon moralism nor upon the threat of divine retribution, but upon the miracle of God's redeeming love revealed in the events of Holy Pascha. The sacraments of the Church offer the proper context for such preaching, for they are the unique channels of communion through which God's saving grace is made accessible to the faithful and through which the faithful respond to that grace in an attitude of unceasing repentance and praise.[3]

Another action that gives the impression that preaching is not part of the Liturgy is what some priests do before proceeding to the pulpit to deliver the sermon. They remove the chasuble and wear a black robe. This act is like a signal that the Liturgy is being interrupted by something that is clearly not a part of it, i.e., the sermon.

The enormity of the preacher's responsibility in the act of preaching is apparent when we realize that each time he addresses a congregation of five hundred people, his twelve-minute sermon takes one hundred hours of their combined time. Such a responsibility demands a priority of the preacher's time in preparation.

A bishop once spoke to a group of theological students. He began by saying to them, "Stand up." Everyone rose to their feet. After a moment he said, "Now sit down." The audience, somewhat puzzled, obediently sat down.

"I hope you get the point," he said. "Words cause things to happen."

---

[3]   From a sermon preached to the Holy Synod of the Ecumenical Patriarchate. Translated from *Episkepsis*, 162 (February, 1977).

God uses words to cause things to happen. People may not always heed God's word, but that does not take away from its effectiveness. His is a saving word for all who respond to it with faith.

Preaching has always been one of the primary means by which the Holy Spirit has worked, and is working, to renew the life of the Church. Herein also lies its priority.

Thus, the priority of preaching established by Jesus, lived out in the ministry of the early apostles and the Church Fathers, incorporated into the very Liturgy itself, calls on us to "preach the word...in season and out of season" (2 Tim 4.2) "rightly handling the word of truth" (2 Tim 2.15). At the close of the anaphora or eucharistic canon, the priest commemorates the holy Orthodox patriarchs and the local bishop, beseeching God to "grant them for your holy churches...to rightly define the word of your truth." Thus preserving and proclaiming the faith "once delivered to the saints" through the medium of preaching occupies a central role in the divine economy of salvation.

Preaching as a Sacrament

Why is preaching not a sacrament?

It certainly has the necessary scriptural authority: "Go therefore and teach all nations" (Mt 28.19); "Go and proclaim the kingdom of God" (Lk 9.60); "Preach the word; be instant in season, out of season; reprove, rebuke, exhort, be unfailing in patience and in teaching" (2 Tim 4.2); "And every day in the temple and at home they did not cease teaching and preaching Jesus as the Christ" (Acts 5.42); "For we cannot but speak of what we have seen and heard" (Acts 4.20); "And when they had prayed, the place in which they were gathered together was shaken; and they were filled with the Holy Spirit and spoke the word of God with boldness" (Acts 4.31).

Who says preaching is not a sacrament?

The Orthodox Church has never limited the number of sacraments to seven. No less an authority on liturgical theology than Fr. Alexander Schmemann has said, "The proclamation of the word is a sacramental act *par excellence* because it is a transforming act. It transforms the man who hears the word into a receptacle of the word and a temple of the Holy Spirit."[4] Preaching is a sacrament by which the word of God through the Holy Spirit brings to us the real presence of God. An outstanding church historian, Jarsolav Pelikan, calls its "the audible sacrament."

To be effective, preaching must be sacramental. It must be an act prolonging the great act of the Incarnation through which the Son of God continues his ministry of preaching the kingdom through his ordained apostles.

In the Eucharist the word is acted out but is not a silent word. Scripture readings and the sermon always accompany the celebration of the Eucharist. Proceeding from the Eucharist and leading to it, the sermon becomes the sacrament of the word.

Metropolitan Constantine (Pringiponessos) has written:

> Word and sacrament, then, cannot be viewed as separate components of Christian life that function independently of one another. Divorced from the

---

4   Alexander Schmemann, *For the Life of the World* (Crestwood, N.Y., 1975).

word, the sacrament is reduced to a self-sufficient ritual, regarded as effective in and of itself; and thus it comes perilously close to magic. Divested of its proper sacramental context, the word becomes an object to be analyzed rather than a subject—a person—to be encountered and worshiped.[5]

Coming as it does in the Liturgy following the reading of two Scripture lessons, the power of the Scriptures should flow directly into the power of the sermon so that the congregation experiences the two as one.

As a sacramental, preaching is not just a priest speaking. It is a divine-human encounter. It is God continuing to reveal himself in Christ, seeking the lost, healing the broken, lifting the fallen, bringing the dead to life. It is God in Christ calling all to join him in loving toil for the kingdom.

One of the greatest victories in the history of Christianity occurred following Peter's sermon at Pentecost. Yet the victory was not solely the result of Peter's preaching. It was the Holy Spirit using Peter's sermon as the instrument for his coming in great power. And so it has been through the ages. Whenever preaching is inspired by the Holy Spirit, it has continued to produce a new awareness of the reality of the presence and power of God among his people. Such preaching has always been a sacrament, a means of grace, bringing sinners to repentance and increasing faith.

What is Preaching?

Saint Irenaios said, "The glory of God is man become fully alive, but the life of man is the vision of God." It is the

---

[5]   From a sermon preached to the Holy Synod of the Ecumenical Patriarchate. Translated from *Episkepsis* 162 (February, 1977).

preacher's task to hold up before us the vision of God that brings life.

Preaching is a continuation of the process of religious persuasion begun by the apostles—a process that once wooed the world away from its pagan values.

The basic meaning of the Greek word *kyrex* is 'herald,' one who announces the message of another in authority. In the strict New Testament use of the word, *kyressein* does not mean the delivery of a learned discourse in well-chosen words and a pleasant voice. It is the declaration of an event. It proclaims a happening; the happening is the good news of a new saving relationship between God and man in the life, work, death and resurrection of Jesus.

When asked to write a poem, Carl Sandburg said, "Ordering a man to write a poem is like commanding a pregnant woman to give birth to a red-headed baby. You can't do it. It is an act of God." Though not entirely in the same sense, preaching is an act of God, an act of prayer, an act of divine inspiration. It is God speaking through us.

Halford Luccock, who taught preaching at Yale, said once, "the aim of preaching is not the elucidation of a subject, but the transformation of a person."

Preaching at its finest is the word of God directed to the real needs of people so that people are led to faith, and from faith to glorifying God in praise and thanksgiving.

Preaching is nothing less than God in Christ coming to us again in disguise as he did in Bethlehem. Now he comes through a poor, unworthy priest to proclaim his saving word. Often we fail to recognize the gift because it comes wrapped in a weak person. The words of Jesus are perennially true: "If you knew the gift of God, and who it is that is saying to you, 'Give me a drink,' then I would not be obliged to run after you and beg for a drink. You would run after me and ask me for the living water. But since you do not know the gift and do not recognize him who is speaking with you, you despise me" (Jn 4.10-11).

Preaching is not a throne of eloquence, but an opportunity to grapple with human lives. Preaching is "an engineering operation by which a chasm is bridged so that spiritual goods on one side—'the unsearchable riches of Christ'—are actually transported into personal lives upon the other."[6]

The purpose of preaching is "not merely to discuss repentance, but to persuade people to repent; not merely to debate the meaning and possibility of Christian faith, but to produce

Christian faith in the lives of...listeners; not merely to talk about the available power of God to bring victory over trouble and temptation, but to send people out from their worship on Sunday with victory in their possession. A preacher's task is to create in his congregation the thing he is talking about."[7] Preaching is to confront people in their present condition with the affirmations and demands of the Christian gospel.

Saint Basil compares the messengers of the gospel and their words to arrows sharpened through the power of the Holy Spirit: "The arrows, falling in the hearts of those who were at some time enemies of the King, draw them to

---

[6]   Harry E. Fosdick, *The Living of These Days* (New York, 1946).

[7]   Ibid.

a love of truth, draw them to the Lord, so that they who were enemies to God are reconciled to him through its teachings."[8]

Preaching is like an icon: it is a reflection of celestial glory. "Preach in order to pray," said Abraham Heschel. "Preach in order to inspire others to pray. The test of a good sermon is that it can be converted to prayer."[9]

The purpose of preaching is that "Christ be formed in you...that he dwell in your hearts by faith" (Gal 4.19 and Eph 3.17).

Preaching has a perpendicular dimension. It is God speaking from above to man below. The prophets expressed this by repeatedly saying, "Thus saith the Lord." Every other form of speech is horizontal by nature: man speaking to man. In preaching the horizontal is derived from the perpendicular.

Preaching is like the spark plug in a motor. It is the source of motivation, inspiration and activity. From the pulpit sounds the clarion call to action. Men are brought to repentance. Faith is increased. Vision is seen. Work is done. A world is conquered for Christ.

Preaching is not the giving of good advice, but the sharing of good news. It is not the giving of an editorial, but the proclamation of God's truth in Christ. It is not a dialogue between preacher and people, but a dialogue between God and man. Saint John Chrysostom, in his book *On the Priesthood*, described the preaching of the word of God as "an instrument of healing." Preaching is a theoph-

---

8   In his commentary on the Psalms.

9   A. Heschel, *Man's Quest for God* (New York, 1954).

any, a continuing manifestation of Christ in every liturgy as proclaimed by the little entrance. The gospel book, held up high, announces the coming of Christ to reveal himself to us both through his word as well as in the breaking of the bread.

St. Basil writes that preaching is a charisma (gift) of the Holy Spirit, a sacred ministry (*leitourgia*) to be executed in the Christian community for the benefit of others.[10]

During the Second World War a courier service was developed from occupied Norway to neutral Sweden. Bishop Odd Hagen of Norway was one of the couriers who, at the risk of his own life, carried concealed messages across the Norwegian border into Sweden, where they could safely be relayed to the intelligence services of the Allies. He once described his work as follows: "We did not read the messages," he said. "We did not tamper with them or alter them. That was not our commission. Our sole task was to deliver messages composed by others. We were not asked to be original or imaginative. We were only asked to be faithful. We were to hand on a message as it had been handed to us."

This is the message the Orthodox preacher is called to deliver untampered, as so well expressed by these words used every year on the Sunday of Orthodoxy:

> As the prophets beheld, as the apostles have taught,
> as the Church has received, as the teachers have
> dogmatized, as the universe has agreed, as grace has

---

[10]   Paul J. Fedwick, *The Church and the Charisma of Leadership in Basil of Caesarea*, Pontifical Institute of Medieval Studies (Toronto, 1979).

shown forth, as truth has revealed, as falsehood has
been dissolved, as wisdom has presented, as Christ
has awarded!

Thus we declare, thus we assert, thus we preach.
Christ our true God: in words, in writings, in
thoughts, in sacrifices, in churches, in holy icons.
Thus we honor his saints: worshiping and reverenc-
ing Christ as God and Lord, and honoring his saints
as true servants of the same Lord of all, accordingly
offering them veneration.

This is the faith of the apostles, this is the faith of the
Fathers, this is the faith of the Orthodox, this is the
faith which has established the Ecoumene.

Preaching is a reincarnation of the word of God. When
the priest mounts the pulpit, the word of God becomes
flesh again.

In the 1956 Warrack Lectures, David Maclennan por-
trayed preaching as almost the only "head-on confrontation with God that most people will ever experience." He
says that preaching "is to lead them to that collision with
reality through which God speaks most clearly, most personally and most decisively." Preaching is not an address
before a meeting. It is bound by a scriptural text. It un-
dertakes to proclaim eternal truth in the name of God, to
herald God's saving grace in Christ, to transform lives.

Phillips Brooks said, "Preaching is a movement from
the presence of Christ to the presence of people."

To preach is to obey Christ's command: "Feed my
sheep."

The goal of preaching is not to catch the spirit of the age, but to correct it with God's truth. The preacher is a thermostat, not a thermometer.

The purpose of preaching is to humble the sinner, to exalt the Savior and to produce saintly lives by the grace of the Holy Spirit.

The preacher is to so present Christ that people will come to know him, love him, serve him and yield their lives to him.

The purpose of preaching is to write God's message in the hearts of people. "You yourselves are our letter of recommendation, written on your hearts, to be known and read by all men; and you show that you are a letter from Christ delivered by us, written not with ink, but with the spirit of the living God, not on tablets of stone, but on tablets of human hearts" (2 Cor 3.2-3).

Some years ago in England the king was on the radio. In the middle of his speech, an electrical wire broke, preventing his voice from being carried to those who were listening. Realizing there was no time to fix anything, an alert workman in the studio took the two wire ends in his hands and became himself a part of the circuit, allowing the king's speech to continue.

I can think of no better definition of the priest's role in preaching. He becomes a living circuit between God and man, allowing the King's message to pass through him to God's people.

Saint Basil says that those who proclaim the gospel are the lips and the eyes of the body of Christ. As lips they lend their voices to the Holy Spirit in order that he may write "the words of eternal life in the hearts of the faithful"; as eyes their function is to "discern between good and evil and guide the members of Christ toward that which benefits each."[11]

The One Who Preaches

A young priest was walking dejectedly through a park one day. A friend met him and asked, "What on earth is the matter with you? You look hopeless." The priest heaved a long sigh and said, "Chrysostom is dead. Gregory of Nyssa is dead. Basil-all are dead. The responsibility on my shoulders is almost more than I can bear."

The friend replied, "But Jesus is not dead. The Holy Spirit is not dead. The same Holy Spirit who produced Chrysostom and Gregory and Basil can produce new Chrysostoms, new Gregories and new Basils." And he does!

The famous preacher, Phillips Brooks, was right when he said that preaching is truth through personality. The personality through which the truth passes is as important in the communication of the gospel as the truth itself. "The truth must come really through the person, not merely over his lips, not merely into his understanding and out through his pen. It must come through his character, his affections, his whole intellectual and moral being. It must come genuinely through him," said Phillips Brooks.[12] The Gospel is stamped with something of ourselves when we preach it.

---

11   Fedwick, *Basil.*
12   *Lectures on Preaching* (New York, 1898).

Although divine truth never changes, the human personality is constantly changing. This is what makes the Gospel message ever so new and so unique. No two preachers can write the exact same sermon because no two preachers are alike. Each is uniquely different. In fact, even one preacher cannot preach the same sermon twice if he is at all growing.

Fr. Theodore Stylianopoulos has observed, "It is through the preacher that the Gospel can come alive for the listener.... He bridges the gap...between the Bible and the modern listener.... The clarity and power of the Gospel is almost directly related to the evangelical radiance of the preacher himself."[13] The radiance comes from the preacher's own personal conversion to Christ and union with him. Faith can only be transmitted through faith.

Which comes first, thunder or lightning? Sound or light? Lightning (light) comes first; thunder (sound) comes later. So it is that light—the example of a life lived in Christ— must come first. Then must come the sound (preaching). Preaching must be preceded by the life in Christ. To use the words of Saint Basil, "The light must always come before the sound."

If the preacher lives in darkness, confusion and doubt, there will be no saving light. The words will mean nothing. The priest is called not just to preach a sermon, but, in all humility and with relentless ascetic effort and self-discipline, to be a sermon. The Church Fathers compare one who teaches with words, without doing works, to a fig tree which has beautiful leaves but does not bear fruit.

---

[13]   *The Gospel of Christ* (Brookline, Ma., 1981).

Who then can preach the Gospel? [asks Dr. Charles Malik, a noted Orthodox layman and former President of the General Assembly of the United Nations]. I think not any man. He alone can preach the Gospel who is called by God and through whom God can speak. But who is called by God and who is his mouthpiece? Only he to whom the Gospel radically speaks. Only he who allows it to analyze and judge his life. Only he who humbly and silently stands before its amazing story. Only he who confesses the guilt which it imputes to him. Only he who, gratefully accepting Christ's forgiveness, is cleansed of his sin and endowed from on high with the power of the Holy Ghost. Only he who acknowledges that exactly the same forces of darkness which slew our Lord long ago in Jerusalem are as operative in our own lives and times.... He alone can preach the Gospel in such a way that through him.... God speaks.... The power of God, which he is then able to mediate simply, directly and without any effort on his part, is absolutely incredible. It is not he who acts, but the Holy Ghost.... Blessed are those who are called to this greatest of all honors."[14]

Saint Basil writes that those who preach lend their voices to the Holy Spirit so that he may write words of eternal life in the hearts of the faithful. He calls them fathers and nurses since they beget new members for the Church. Those who preach, continues Saint Basil, lead the disciples of Christ "to the blooming and fragrant nourishment of spiritual doctrine, water them with living water with

---

[14]   Charles Malik, *Christ and Crisis* (Grand Rapids, Mich., 1962).

the concurrent assistance of the Holy Spirit, raise them up and nourish them until they produce fruit; then they guide them to rest and safety from those who lay snares to them."[15]

In order not to impede the word of God from becoming a fountain of living water, springing up to life everlasting in the hearts of the faithful, Saint Basil has these words of caution for the preacher. Most of these come from his Moral Rule 70:

> 1. That we must not use the word of teaching in an ostentatious or huckstering way, flattering the hearers and satisfying our own pleasures or needs; but we must be such men as speak for the glory of God in his presence.

> 2. That the leader of the word must not abuse his authority (iexousia) to insult those who are under him, nor even exalt himself over them, but must rather use his rank as an opportunity for practicing humility towards them.

> 3. That one must not proclaim the gospel by way of contention or envy or irritation against any.

> 4. That one must not use human advantages in proclaiming the gospel, lest the grace of God be obscured thereby.

> 5. That we must not imagine that the successful issue of preaching is secured by our own devices, but trust wholly in God.

---

[15]   *Basil*, (Toronto, 1979).

6. That he who is entrusted with the proclamation of the gospel should acquire nothing beyond his own necessities.

7 That as regards care for worldly things, a man must not put himself at the disposal of those who pay undue attention to them.

8. That those who, in order to please their hearers, neglect to declare God's will boldly, enslaving themselves to those they wish to please, no longer have the Lord for their master.[16]

A Great Occupational Hazard

One of the great occupational hazards of the priesthood is pride. Yet nowhere is pride more incongruous and unpardonable than in the servant of the cross. Chrysostom speaks of Christian preachers who imitated, and even surpassed, the Greek rhetoricians in their eagerness for praise. Chrysostom stated that if they won the praise of the congregation, they were as happy as if they had gained a kingdom; but if their discourse ended in silence, their despondency was unbearable. Some went so far as to have hirelings in the audience to begin the applause!

To show how shallow and meaningless applause and praise are when directed to the sermon, let me share with you the parable of the preaching goose:

The Danish theologian Kierkegaard once told a homely parable about a flock of geese that milled around in a filthy barnyard imprisoned by a high wooden fence. One day a preaching goose landed in the barnyard. Faithful to his

---

[16]   Fedwick, *Basil.*

calling, he stepped onto an old crate and began to preach. He castigated the geese for being satisfied to live in that small, smelly barnyard when God had given them wings with which to fly in the trackless wastes of the sky. He spoke of the goodness of God in giving the geese wings. He urged them to use their wings to fly out of the barnyard to better surroundings. This pleased the geese. They nodded their heads in approval and commented on what a great preacher the goose was. They marveled at what he had said and applauded his eloquence. All this they did. But one thing they never did. They did not use their wings to leave the barnyard. They went right back to their old accustomed haunts.

The best compliment that can be paid to any sermon is a changed life. This is clearly something we cannot accomplish—only God. We sow the seed, but only God can give the growth. Every sermon must be bracketed with prayer, for only God can prepare the soil in men's hearts for the effective and fruitful reception of the seed of God's word.

An archbishop once preached a magnificent sermon. A friend ran up to him in order to be the first to congratulate him. He managed to get there before anyone else. "Your Eminence, your sermon was magnificent. Thank you!"

"Thank you!" said the archbishop. "You were the second one to thank me for the sermon this morning."

"But I was the first. In fact, I ran all the way up here to make sure I was the first."

"No, you were the second one to come. The devil was here first, before you."

If a sermon attracts too much attention to the preacher, it has failed its purpose. The purpose of every sermon is to focus attention on Jesus, not the preacher. The best compliment is not, "I heard a great sermon, but, "I met a great God"; it is not, "What a great sermon," but, "What a great gospel."

There are two ways to preach. The first is to stand in front of the cross and call attention to yourself. The second is to keep behind the cross, to stay out of sight and call attention to the One on the cross.

We need to get ourselves out of the way. Saint John the Baptist said, "He must increase; I must decrease." Jesus "did not count equality with God a thing to be grasped, but emptied himself taking the form of a servant" (Phil 2.6-7). Every priest is a servant—a servant of him "who, though he was in the form of God," became a servant. We need to realize that if the priest is anything, he is the donkey which brought Christ to Jerusalem. It is our task to bring Christ to our people. There is a story according to which the donkey on Palm Sunday was quite proud because he thought the crowds were applauding him. If the people are waving palms and applauding, they are cheering not the donkey, but the Christ. Aesop wrote a fable about a fly perched on the wheel of a furiously racing chariot. The fly surveyed the enveloping clouds of dense dust and remarked, "Lo, see what dust I am raising!"

A biographer of Michaelangelo tells us that one of the problems with which he grappled was keeping his own shadow off the statue on which he was working. He found that in the most intricate work he was handicapped by his own shadow. So he devised a miner's lamp to use on his forehead. Thus he eliminated the shadow of himself and was able to work in full illumination. If there is anything that serves as a handicap to the pastor, it is the shadow of himself. The self protrudes so persistently that the view of the Son of God is obstructed. We must get out of the way to let the world see Jesus. We must pray daily for God's grace to enable us to keep the shadow of our ego out of our preaching.

People come to church to hear Jesus—not us. I once preached at a pulpit that had this verse carved into it on the preacher's side where he could see it constantly: "Sir, I would see Jesus"—Jesus, not the talents or the wisdom of the preacher! When after Herod's speech the people said, "It is the voice of a god, not of a man," Herod fell dead. Popularity—or rather pride—is a dangerous thing, especially in the preacher.

A person was once led to recommit his life to Jesus following a particularly moving sermon. When asked who the preacher was, he replied that he had no idea who the preacher was; he only knew that the Lord Jesus had spoken to him very personally that morning. That is always the mark of a truly effective sermon. It brings the listener face to face not with the preacher, but with Jesus.

A good antidote to pride for excellency of preaching is to remember that our Lord calls great not him who preaches the word of God, but him who practices first and then preaches. "He who does them and teaches them [the commandments] shall be called great in the kingdom of heaven" (Mt 5.19). How woefully short we fall in the area of practice! How humble this should keep us!

When the famous orchestral conductor Toscanini was applauded by his orchestra after practicing one of Beethoven's symphonies, he said to them, "Gentlemen, I am nothing. You are nothing. Beethoven is everything." His duty was not to call attention to himself or to his orchestra; his duty was to obliterate himself and his orchestra and to let Beethoven flow through. That is the duty and task of the preacher.

As Father Nadim Tarazi has written, "As preacher, he [the Orthodox priest] is to concentrate on God's word, studying it, preparing his sermon in tears when the text is judging him, and—unworthy though he be—approach the pulpit as he would the chalice and there speak out. He is to do all this so that not his voice, but God's word is heard, not his weakness, but God's power is preached while he— this time a listener of the word together with his parishioners—is challenged by each word coming out of his own mouth! And both preacher and parishioners, heeding not their own thoughts and feelings, but the Lord's word, will grow into a living image of the Most High!"[17]

"Therefore, my dear brothers, stand firm. Let nothing move you. Always give yourselves fully to the work of the Lord, knowing that in the Lord your labor is not in vain (1 Cor 15.58).

---

[17]   J.J. Allen, ed., *Orthodox Synthesis* (Crestwood, N.Y., 1981).

2
The Content of Our Preaching

Christian ministers are not supposed to preach their private opinions, at least from the pulpit...They are expected to propagate and to sustain 'the faith which was once delivered unto the saints'....One has to be sure that one is preaching the same Gospel that was delivered and that one is not introducing instead any 'strange Gospel' of his own...I am going to preach...the message of salvation, as it has been handed down to me by an uninterrupted tradition of the Church Universal. I would not isolate myself in my own age... 'In a time such as this one' one has to preach the *whole Christ*, Christ and the Church—totus Christus, caput et corpus, to use the famous phrase of St. Augustine.[18]

Religious News Service (RNS) carried a story some time ago of a French student's criticism of the content of sermons in Catholic churches. He suggested the faithful are hungering for sermons on God and the supernatural and not 'trendy' sermons on everyday affairs.

---

[18]   G. Florovsky, *The Bible, Church, Tradition: An Eastern Orthodox View* (Belmont, Ma., 1972).

He was critical of five sermons he had heard in as many weeks. The first dealt with 'communal regrouping', the second with 'the spirit of the (summer) holidays/ In the third the people were invited to speak from the 'top of their heads.' The fourth was a summary of a recent French comedy. And the fifth developed the theory that 'capitalism and fraternal life were incompatible.'

The student suggested such a trend was dangerous because parish priests are treating less and less what people come to church to hear. He said that when he comes to church, he expects to have his faith shaken a bit and have the priests talk to him about God and "Christian revelation." He couldn't care less what the reverend father thinks about changes in government.

He also stated that the desire of priests to appear "in vogue" or "latched on to life" is a "very bad thing." "Man aspires for eternity," he said.

Listen for a moment to what the content of Saint Paul's preaching was: "For what we preach is not ourselves, but Jesus Christ as Lord, with ourselves as your servants for Jesus' sake" (2 Cor 4.5).

Examining the content of ninety sermons on the Gospel of Saint Matthew, it was discovered that "Chrysostom spoke forty times on alms giving alone; he spoke some thirteen times on poverty, more than thirty times on avarice, and about twenty times against wrongly acquired and wrongly used wealth—all in all, ninety or a hundred sermons on the social themes of poverty and wealth."[19]

---

[19] Chrysostomus Baur, *John Chrysostom and His Time 1* (Westminster, Md., 1959-60).

As he preached through the Gospel of Matthew, Saint Chrysostom related it directly to the personal and social problems of his day. The content of his preaching was God's word speaking to man's problems.

Saint Basil counsels that the preacher should be able to say, "I bring back to you the tidings the Spirit taught me, and I say nothing of my own, nothing human." The content of Saint Basil's preaching was not human wisdom, but the good news.

It has been said that Saint Paul made a great mistake when he preached to the philosophers in Athens. He spoke about Providence. He spoke about the government of the universe. He spoke about Creation. He spoke about the Resurrection, but he never mentioned the name of Christ. He never mentioned the cross. That may be why when he wrote the letter to Corinth, he resolved to preach, "From now on, nothing but Christ and him crucified." The content of Saint Paul's preaching changed dramatically after Athens. It is interesting that he never went back to Athens or wrote a letter there. As one writer says:

> Paul spoke here [in Athens] as a philosopher, arguing on a philosophical level, not as a bearer of [good] news. The expectation of those who listened to him was precisely intellectual curiosity; they were interested in ideas. Paul was adding to their knowledge; they were curious and they listened...some laughed at him, rejecting his message as unverified.... Paul learned his lesson; and in writing to the Corinthians he approached them differently. For he wrote that Christ sent him 'to preach the good news, and not to preach that in terms of philosophy in which the Cru-

cifixion of Christ cannot be expressed. The language of the cross may be illogical to those who are not on the way to salvation, but those of us who are on the way see it as God's power to save' (1 Cor 1.17-18). Here Paul was announcing the news of Jesus' death and resurrection and the power of God to save all through acceptance of Jesus And his message bore fruit.[20]

Preaching the good news has a power to save which the teaching of philosophy can never have. The content of our preaching is not philosophy, but good news.

Regarding the content of preaching, Saint Chrysostom chastised the preachers of his day who gave their hearers what they wanted to hear rather than what they needed to hear. He writes:

> We [preachers] act like a father who gives a sick child a cake or an ice, or something else that is merely nice to eat—just because he asks for it—and who takes no pain to give him what is good for him; and then when the doctors blame him he says, 'I could not bear to hear my child cry.' That is what we do when we elaborate beautiful sentences, fine combinations and harmonies, to please but not to profit and not to better your conduct.

It was Chrysostom's custom to preach through the books of the Bible, taking a short verse as the subject of each sermon. Today there survive no less than ninety of his sermons on Saint Matthew's Gospel. He favored the Epistles of Saint Paul and preached straight through al-

---

[20] Fr. Schmidt S.J., "Another Look at Christian Preaching," *Worship* 55, no. 5 (September, 1981).

most all of them. Rather than being attracted by Paul's theology and grace, Chrysostom preached on the Christian life, endeavoring to lead his hearers to the way of holiness and to the life of Christ. Ordained into the priesthood in 386, for the next eleven years he preached his way through most of the New Testament and parts of the Old. He remains, to this day, one of the greatest examples of true biblical preaching. Hans von Campenhausen writes, "The homilies of Chrysostom are probably the only ones from the whole of Greek antiquity which, at least in part, are still readable today as Christian sermons   They are so ethical, so simple and so clear-headed."

To each preacher the Church would say today, as in every age, "Go, preach with courage not what they 'hire' you to say, but what God has sent you to declare."[21]

Types of Preaching

Let us look briefly at the types of preaching that existed in the early Church:

1. *Kerygma.* This is a proclamation or announcement without argument. It is the plain statement of what we believe as Christians. It simply says, "This is what we believe" without trying to justify or defend it. Pheidippides ran from Marathon to Athens to deliver the announcement (*kerygma*): "Rejoice! We have won!"

Two other words belong with *kerysso*, 'to proclaim like a herald.' These words are *evangelizomai*, 'to tell the good news,' and *martyro*, 'to bear witness.' We are telling the

---

[21]   Hans von Campenhausen, *The Fathers of the Greek Church* (New York, 1959).

good news with the authority of a royal herald, but the message is also a part of our lives. Whereas the ancient herald merely shouted what was given to him, we are sharing what is real and personal to us. The message is a part of the messenger because the messenger is a witness, *martys*. God wants the herald to be a witness as well. The apostles were aware of this: "For we cannot but speak the things which we have seen and heard" (Acts 4.20); "For you will be a witness for him to all men of what you have seen and heard" (Acts 22.15).

2. *Didache.* This is the Greek word for teaching. *Didache* is the explanation of that which was proclaimed (*kerygma*). The Sermon on the Mount is an example of didache. We must remember, however, that *didache* must be preceded by the *kerygma* since its purpose is to explain in a systematic way the implications of the *kerygma*.

3. *Paraklesis.* This is an exhortation to accept the Christian faith and live the Christian life. Again, *paraklesis* must be preceded by both *kerygma* and *didache* since there is no point in exhorting a person to accept a faith in which he has not been instructed.

4. *Homilia.* This is a general discussion of any subject in the light of the Christian faith. Yet, again we realize that in order for *homilia* to be effective, it has to be preceded by *didache*. The hearer must be grounded in the content of the Christian Gospel before *homilia* can achieve its goal.

If we examine preaching today, we discern a vast amount of the *homilia* type, i.e., a general treatment of almost any subject under the sun from a supposedly Christian point of view. We find also a great amount of *parak-*

lesis preaching of the Christian pep-talk variety. Yet both these types of preaching become extremely shallow and flounder because they lack a strong root system. They are not preceded by *kerygma* and *didache,* by a systematic and planned explanation of the Christian faith. We end up exhorting people and talking to them (*homilia*) about a faith they really do not understand.

Speaking of the lack of *didache* in contemporary preaching, Father George Florovsky wrote:

> In the early Church the preaching was emphatically theological. It was not a vain speculation. The New Testament itself is a theological book. Neglect of theology in the instruction given to laity in modern times is responsible both for the decay of personal religion and for that sense of frustration which dominates the modern mood...because no theology is usually preached, they [the laity] adopt some 'strange theologies' and combine them with the fragments of traditional beliefs. The whole appeal of the 'rival gospels' in our days is that they offer some sort of pseudo-theology, a system of pseudo-dogmas. They are gladly accepted by those who cannot find any theology in the reduced Christianity of 'modern' style. That existential alternative which many face in our days has been aptly formulated by an English theologian, 'Dogma or...death.' The age of a-dogmatism and pragmatism has closed. And, therefore, the ministers of the Church have to preach again doctrines and dogmas—the word of God.[22]

---

[22]   Florovsky, *Bible, Church, Tradition.*

Teaching Sermons

The need for teaching sermons (*didache*) from the pulpit has always been immense. On any given Sunday, a large proportion of the congregation consists of people already committed to Christ, who are trying to figure out exactly what is required of them by that commitment. A series of sermons on the Nicene Creed or the Beatitudes or the Lord's Prayer would not only prevent the preacher from searching frantically for a subject on which to preach, but would help ground his people in the faith once delivered to the saints. It is a great error for any preacher to overestimate his congregation's familiarity with even the most basic teachings of the Christian faith.

Speaking on the importance of teaching theology in our sermons, the members of the Orthodox Consultation on "Preaching and Teaching the Christian Faith Today" stated:

For centuries theology was thought of as an exclusively clerical task. But the time has come for a 'declericalization' of theology. If theology is, above all, the study of the saving Truth, it is needed by all members of the Church, [it] is their essential spiritual food. To become this, however, it must revise its language, forms, methods, be made into a common concern of the Church.[23]

The content of our preaching is often trivial. In the Middle Ages a sermon was once preached on the neatly folded napkin found by the tomb of the risen Christ. The

---

[23] "Orthodox Consultation on Preaching and Teaching the Christian Faith Today," St. *Vladimir's Theological Quarterly* 25, no. 2 (1981).

topic of the sermon was that we ought to be neat and not throw things around at home!!

Halford Luccock, who taught preaching at Yale, put these words once in the mouth of a parishioner:

> I went to church yesterday and have been groping in the fog ever since. It was a good service; the hymns were good; the Lord's Prayer was good—I have always approved of it. But the sermon was a series of skillful maneuvers in a vacuum. It reminded me of a can of coffee on the shelf at home, on which it says Vacuum packed'   The statements up in the stratosphere and not a single raindrop came down to water the earth.[24]

Improve the Feed

The content of our preaching must come down from God's stratosphere as refreshing raindrops to the parched souls of God's people. A farmer told a minister that he noticed the topic of a recent preachers' conference was "How To Get More People To Come to Church." He went on to say that when farmers get together, they never discuss how to get the cattle to come to be fed; but they spend their time studying how to improve the feed.

We need to spend much time on trying "to improve the feed" by concentrating on the content of the sermon. When people are hungry, we don't give them a menu, but real food. One of the great preachers of our time, James S. Stewart, has written a masterful study on the specific subject of the content of preaching which is highly recom-

---

[24]   Halford Luccock, *Living Without Gloves* (New York, 1957).

mended. Its title is *A Faith To Proclaim*. The author demon-strates how the great themes of the Christian faith, i.e., Incarnation, Redemption, Trinity, etc., can be preached effectively to people today.[25]

The Need for Repetition

It is important to remember the constant need to keep repeating and reminding our people of the eternal truths of our faith which are so quickly forgotten. The Church Fathers incorporated these truths into the liturgical year so that we may be reminded of them annually. Much in the content of the faith we are called to preach must take the form of repetition, for the need to remember is great. *Kerygma* and *didache* are not always the introduction of new truths as much as the reminding of truths we already know and tend so easily to forget. We need to be reminded more than informed. For time is like an eraser that comes and wipes clean the slate of memory.

'Come' and 'Go'

Another factor that we need to watch in the content of our preaching is the need for a balance between the "Come unto me ail you who labor and are heavy laden and I will give you rest" and the other words of Jesus, "Go into the world...." I remember preaching a sermon once on the beautiful word 'come' as it was used by Jesus to invite people to himself for forgiveness, comfort, eternal life, peace, etc. As I examined this sermon years later, I realized that the 'come' should have been balanced with

---

25   James Stewart, *A Faith To Proclaim* (Grand Rapids, Mich., 1972).

the 'go' of Jesus. We come to Jesus that we may go. We may come to be transfigured with Jesus on the Mount of Transfiguration, but we may not pitch our tent and stay there. We must go back down into the valley, as Jesus did, to heal the sick, feed the poor and raise the dead. We come to Jesus as 'disciples' (learners) that we may be sent into the world as 'apostles' (ones who are sent). First we come, then we go. Often our sermons have too many 'come's' and not enough 'go's.' We can also have too many 'go's' and not enough 'come's.' There needs to be a balance in the content of our preaching between the call to prayer and the call to action. The personal gospel and the social gospel are really one gospel. They belong together.

Speaking of the importance of verbs like 'come' and 'go' in Christian preaching, Halford Luccock wrote:

> When someone asked Mr. Averill Harriman, the veteran of so many European conferences, how his French was, he said, 'My French is excellent, all except the verbs.' Quite an exception! If often happens that our Christianity is excellent, 'all except the verbs.' The nouns are wonderful—Master, Savior, Redeemer. The adjectives are inspiring—noble, divine, sacred. The verbs are often missing. No action. Yet the verb is the sinew of speech. It is the sinew of the Gospel, great verbs—come, go, follow, serve, give, love, share. [26]

After having 'come' to the Liturgy and received Christ in the Eucharist, we are invited to 'go' back in the world to continue and fulfill the work that Jesus began. This is the 'liturgy after the Liturgy,' the 'go' after the 'come.'

---

[26]   Halford Luccock, *Communicating the Gospel* (New York, 1954).

'You Must' Preaching

There has always been too much of the 'you must' type of preaching. This is the preaching that keeps telling us how we must act as Christians without once telling us how to do it. It is preaching that assumes a simplistic view of human nature. It operates on the level of humanism, namely, just tell people what to do and they will have no problem on their own living up to what God expects of them.

It is true that Jesus used this type of preaching, but he never divorced it from God's grace and power. The Beatitudes, for example, are for those who have committed themselves totally to Jesus and live in the Spirit. It is impossible to live the Beatitudes if one is not in the Spirit, filled with the fullness of God's power. The 'oughts' that Saint Paul speaks of in his Epistles proceed from the 'new creation', the new life we receive in Christ, the new presence and power within us.

The Ten Commandments are certainly not ten suggestions. They are 'oughts'. Yet they are set within the framework of God's gracious deliverance of Israel from Egyptian bondage. As a result, the ten 'oughts' become gracious 'oughts', i.e., "I want to do what God commands me because of the new life I have received through his gracious love." In the words of D. J. Randolph, "Love that happens to you creates its own oughtness within you."

Two general rules for preaching are:

1. The 'ought' or 'must' must not stand by itself. It should be preceded by God's grace as in Saint Paul when he writes, "Be kind to one another, tender-

hearted, forgiving one another, even as God has in Christ forgiven you" (Eph 4.32).

2. Every sermon must show how to carry out the 'must'— where and how we receive the power. Thus every sermon must bear testimony to our impotence without Christ and the Holy Spirit abiding in us through faith and the sacraments: "...that Christ may dwell in your hearts through faith...that you may be filled with all the fullness of God" (Eph 3.17)."...you will receive power when the Holy Spirit comes upon you" (Acts 1.8).

I share with you the following brief description, written by Father William Skudlarek, of what the content of our preaching should be:

> The faith to which preaching invites people is the faith that God is actively and lovingly present in their lives, even when, to all appearances, this does not seem to be the case. In other words, it is preaching that proclaims the good news of the great and wonderful things God has done and is doing for his people, rather than preaching that lists do's and don'ts that people must follow if they are to gain the favor of God. The preaching of good news is able to bring us to the recognition that we are loved, that our lives are meaningful, that sources of strength are available to us in this fellowship of faith and love which go beyond anything we might have hoped for. Such preaching helps us see how, in the concrete situations of our lives, we are not caught up in some theater of the absurd, but rather that we are partners with God in a universe where the forces of truth, love and justice that overcame sin and death in the

person of Jesus Christ are now at work in the world
in and through all who are joined with him in faith
and baptism.[27]

It is, indeed, a great Gospel we are called to preach. Yet
we must remember that Jesus is greater than anything we
have ever said or can ever say about him. We can never
say all that there is to say about God no matter how many
years we preach.

There will always be more—far more—to be said. Yet
preach we must, as dying men to dying men, for he has
entrusted us—earthen vessels though we be—with the
words of everlasting life.

Saint Paul defined the content of his preaching as
follows:

> When I came to you, brethren, I did not come pro-
> claiming to you the testimony of God in lofty words
> or wisdom. For I decided to know nothing among
> you except Christ and him crucified. And I was with
> you in weakness and in much fear and trembling;
> and my speech and my message were not in plau-
> sible words of wisdom, but in demonstration of the
> Spirit and power, that your faith might not rest in
> the wisdom of men, but in the power of God (1 Cor
> 2.1-5).

Be Positive

It is far more effective if we are positive in the way we
present the content of our preaching. Chastising and cas-
tigating people for their sins is not as effective as holding

---

[27]   William Skudlarek, O.S.B., *The Word in Worship* (Nashville, 1981).

up before them positive and inspiring examples of how
the Christian faith has worked in the lives of other saints.
People are attracted to goodness and are inspired to live
up to great examples of virtue and holiness. A well-paint-
ed word picture, parable, or life story of how one saint acted in a particular situation will get more results than the
crack of a whip or the constant use of you 'must' do this or
that. Did not Jesus give us a great positive example of what
man is called to be by His own life? Is not this why the
Church holds up before us the lives of the saints? Did not
the apostle John say that Jesus came not to condemn the
world, but to save the world? Who can ever forget the parable of the loving father so mis-appropriately named the
parable of the prodigal son? Was not the content of Jesus'
first sermon positive? "The Spirit of the Lord is upon me
because he has anointed me; he has sent me to announce
good news to the poor, to proclaim release for prisoners
and recovery of sight for the blind" (Lk 4.18).

To be sure, Jesus did condemn on occasion. Like a
building inspector who condemns a building that is about
to collapse as unsafe for human beings to live and work
in, Jesus did condemn, especially the hardened Pharisees;
but his ultimate aim was not to condemn, but to save, to
redeem, rescue, release and renew life.

So it must be in our preaching. It is not enough to condemn adultery; we must hold up before our people a vision of a happy home and show them where to find the
power and the incentive to make one. It is not enough
to condemn alcohol or gambling; we must somehow or
other, by the power Jesus has given us, wean people away
from it to something greater. And we must confront them

constantly with the vision of the 'something greater' for which they were made, their exalted potential, i.e., theosis, to be like Jesus.

Saint Basil describes the content of our preaching in a negative and positive way. Negatively, the preacher of the word should avoid dealing with idle questions (*ta perierga*). He should reject a too sophisticated method of scriptural exegesis and abstain from entering into disputed topics which could harm the simplicity of the Christian faith, for none of these approaches contributes to the edification (*oikodomesis*) of the Church or the salvation of its members. Instead, it should be his concern to provide, through his homilies, spiritual food for his listeners, encouragement and comfort in their struggle against the forces of evil, awareness of their duties and vocation.[28]

E. S. Jones draws an insightful contrast between the preaching of John the Baptist and that of Jesus that points out the importance of preaching the content of our faith in a positive way:

> John the Baptist's first recorded word is, 'You brood of vipers' (Lk 3.7, Moffatt); and Jesus' first recorded word is, 'The Spirit of the Lord is upon me...to preach the gospel to the poor' (Lk 4.18, Moffat). One begins with a suppression, the other with an expression; one with a brood of vipers, the other with a brooding Spirit. One was the gospel of a demand, the other the gospel of an offer; one talked of the coming Wrath/ and the other of 'the coming Kingdom.' John's baptism was with water—to get rid of;

---

28   Skudlarek, O.S.B., *The Word.*

Jesus' baptism was with the Spirit—to get possession
of. One movement died; the other lives on—forever.
John irritated; Jesus inspired.[29]

Some good words to remember in preaching the content of the Christian faith are those uttered by Goethe:
"Treat a man as he is and he remains as he is, but treat
him better than he is and he will become better."

Preach the Cure

A young medical student said to his pastor, "I am studying diseases and I have the symptoms of the diseases I am
studying. I am afraid I will have to drop out of medical
school. I am a nervous wreck." The pastor replied, "Certainly you are studying something beside the disease. You
must be studying cures and remedies and the whole healing process. Why not think beyond the disease to the healing that is possible?"

Every sermon must point beyond the disease of sin, evil
and death to the cure offered by God in Christ. We must
never get so caught up with the problem that we forget the
solution.

A newly ordained clergyman delivered a sermon once
in a small mission church. It was his very first sermon.
After the service he visited an elderly retired clergyman
who happened to be in the congregation that morning.
He asked him how he felt about the sermon. The elderly
preacher was very kind and gentle. He mentioned some of
the good points, then he said, "But you made sin so big and
God so little! Had I not known better, I would have left the

---

[29]   E. S. Jones, *The Way* (Garden City, N.Y., 1978).

church feeling that sin was bigger and stronger than God."
The young preacher never forgot that criticism. He had no
idea that he had made sin bigger than he had made God.

Every sermon should offer people wings to carry them
away from sin, not load them with a greater burden of
guilt.

There are at least two things every sermon should do
for us. First, it should make people aware that they have
sinned. No person should come to the Liturgy on Sunday
morning without seeing the sins of his soul. Second, a sermon ought to point the lost sheep to the safety of the fold,
to the source of forgiveness and power.

The preacher goes to the pulpit not only to tell me where
my problem lies, but even more so to show me where my
solution lies.

Preach Both To Comfort and To Afflict

A baby began to cry during the Sunday morning sermon. The mother began to carry it toward the door. The
high- pitched minister paused and told her, "You need not
leave. The baby is not disturbing me."

Looking back toward the pulpit, the mother replied,
"No, but you are disturbing him."

There is a need in preaching to disturb, for we are called
to comfort the afflicted and afflict the comfortable. Dr. Re-
inhold Neibuhr expressed it well when he wrote in 1953:

> It is very difficult to preach the Gospel honest-
> ly. It means to preach the severity of God to the
> proud, and the mercy of God to the brokenhearted
> A preacher is the mediator of God's judgment and
> also of his mercy...You have to distinguish somewhat

> between those who must be broken before they can
> be rebuilt and those who are broken and must be
> rebuilt, between judgment and mercy.[30]

Good preaching reminds people that they are God's children, but does not let them forget that they are also sinful children needing the Father's forgiveness. God is the one who judges and redeems—not the one or the other, but both. Preaching must reveal both of God's faces. Pascal once said, "Christianity bids man recognize that he is vile, even abominable, and bids him desire to be like God." Preaching which leaves people contented that they are already 'like God' hides from them what they really are.

People come to church because they are wounded by life's sorrows. They need to hear some word of comfort from the Lord. But we need to remember that the word of God is both sweet and bitter, according to Saint John in Revelation 10.8-11. God tells us in John's vision to take the roll (the word of God) from the hand of the angel and to "eat" it, to consume it and digest it so that it becomes part of us. He tells us that the word of God which we consume will be "sweet as honey to the mouth," but "bitter to your stomach." In other words, there is that which comforts us in the word of God, but there is also that which judges and afflicts in order to call us to repentance.

It is true that most people need comfort because they are fighting hard battles in life with fear, insecurity, doubt, temptation. Nevertheless, we need to strive to maintain a balance between judgment and mercy, comfort and affliction. As Cardinal Newman said once, "Christianity is

---

[30]   R. Neibuhr, *Justice and Mercy* (New York, 1974).

a cordial, but no one drinks cordials from morning until night." We need to aim for a vital balance between preaching the grace of God as well as the ethical demands that flow from that grace.

It is exactly because we are called to comfort the afflicted and afflict the comfortable that preaching is a difficult task. We can all understand 'comforting the afflicted,' but the latter sounds a bit harsh. Does God not want us to be comfortable? Of course he does. But when we allow our comfort to insulate us to his call to minister to the needs of our suffering brothers and sisters, then he requires of us a little help in prodding the calloused person out of his affluent comfort to share with those who are in desperate need. When there is injustice and we lie asleep nearby, God requires that someone sound the alarm that will awaken us to the call of justice.

An irate parishioner once said to a pastor, "I come to church to be comforted, and you sound like a fire alarm." The pastor replied, "Perhaps because there is a fire somewhere."

One must be extremely careful not to overdo the 'afflicting' kind of preaching, however, without balancing it with the comfort of God.

When we afflict the comfortable and bring them face to face with God's judgment, we dare not leave them in the depths of guilt and remorse. We must go on to comfort them with the assurance of God's grace and forgiving love.

Listen to a Hasidic tale:

> Long ago in a land beyond the seas, a terrible prophecy was revealed to the king one night through the

magic of the stars: 'The crops of the next harvest will be cursed, and whoever eats of them will go mad.'

At once the king gathered together his wisest advisers from near and far to counsel as to how to meet the approaching calamity. The alternatives were clear: if they ate the food, they would go mad; if they refused to eat, they would die of starvation. Madness or death, which should the choice be?

Many proposals were made by the nobles, but all were rejected. At last, in despair, the king spoke: 'Since there will be no food other than that which is cursed, we have no course but to eat and remain alive. But,' he added, addressing his most faithful counselor, 'I have still enough provisions to save one man. I shall put them in your house so that you may escape the common fate. This will be your duty: when we have all lost our senses, you will ride through the kingdom and in all the streets of the cities, in the shops, the squares, the markets, in the fields before the cottages, you will cry out, "My brothers, my brothers, remember that you are mad." '

Sometimes religion is called to be like the counselor in this story. It must function as a sane man in an insane asylum. It must challenge and oppose the goals of society. It must refuse to adjust. It must afflict a very comfortable society. Saint Anthony referred to this when he wrote, "A time is coming when men will go mad, and when they see someone who is not mad, they will attack him saying, 'Your are mad, you are not like us.' "

A sign which used to stand in front of Saint Patrick's Cathedral said, "Come in and leave your problems here."

This is, indeed, part of the Christian message: to comfort the afflicted. But there should have been another sign beside it to express the other part of the Christian message, a sign that would have read: "Come in and find out what your problems really are to help you deal with them."

Preach the Good News

Christianity is not a Polyanna type religion. It does not begin with good news; it begins by acknowledging the bad news that exists in our world and in our lives: sin, death, suffering, despair, loneliness and hopelessness. Good news cannot be good news unless we first have a sense of the bad news of our situation.

It was into a world full of bad news that Christ came to be our good news. "And the angel said to them [shepherds], 'Be not afraid; for, behold, I bring you good news of a great joy which will come to all people; for to you is born this day in the city of David a Savior, who is Christ the Lord' " (Lk 2.10-11). Mark the words: "good news of a great joy." When Jesus began preaching in Nazareth, he opened to the book of Isaiah and read, "The Spirit of the Lord is upon me because he has anointed me to preach good news to the poor. He has sent me to proclaim release to the captives and recovering of sight to the blind, to set at liberty those who are oppressed, to proclaim the acceptable year of the Lord" (Lk 4.18-19). Then Jesus said to those listening, "Today this scripture has been fulfilled in your hearing" (Lk 4.21). Christ is the fulfillment of God's good news! No wonder Jesus said, "I must preach the good news of the kingdom of God to the other cities also; for I was sent for this purpose" (Lk 4.4-5). We read in Isaiah

52.7, "How beautiful upon the mountains are the feet of him who brings good tidings, who publishes peace...who brings salvation, who says to Zion, 'Your God reigns.'" These prophetic words were fulfilled in Christ.

The whole life and ministry of Jesus in the world is best described by the word *evangelion* or gospel, good news. Saint Mark begins his Gospel: "The beginning of the Gospel of Jesus Christ, the Son of God" (Mk 1.1). Gospel: good news! How hungry modern man is for such good news! When the American Bible Society called its edition of the New Testament *Good News for Modern Man*, it had a runaway best-seller on its hands in less than a month!

GOOD NEWS! Christianity is not a search for God. If it is anything, it is good news from God. It is not man groping and stumbling alone in the darkness, trying to find the ladder to heaven. It is God himself coming down the ladder in his own dear Son that he may lift us out of our blindness and helplessness into his light and power.

Not good advice, but good news; not good views, but good news—this is the Gospel of Christ. It is primarily an announcement of what God does and has done in the person of Jesus. When the early apostles preached, they merely made a proclamation, an announcement of what God had done in Jesus. They called upon the people to listen to the good news: "God was in Christ reconciling the world to himself" (2 Cor 5.19) and making "him to be sin who knew no sin, so that in him we might become the righteousness of God" (2 Cor 5.21). But that was not all. Jesus had risen from the grave. By his death he overcame death for the members of his body, the Church. Then, having ascended into heaven, he sent the gift of the Holy

Spirit upon the early Church, bringing them new life and power, changing their lives completely, filling them with life that was life indeed. That was the message! That was, and is, the Gospel! The entire emphasis is upon what God has done in Christ to overcome man's bad news of sin and death.

There is a beautiful story about the word 'evangelist,' which comes from the Greek word *evangelistes*, one who delivers good news. The word was first used, according to one source, in 490 B.C. at the Battle of Marathon when the Persians had moved their great force toward Athens. The outnumbered Athenians met them twenty-five miles from Athens, fought them in a bitter battle, and finally won the victory. The people of Athens were locked in their city, frightened and trembling, not knowing the outcome of that crucial battle. A messenger, Pheidippides by name, was sent to bring the good news to Athens. Pheidippides ran every step of the way; and when he arrived, his message was this, "*Chairete, nenikamen!*" "Rejoice, we have conquered!"

This, and none other, is the message of the Gospel of Christ, "Rejoice, we have won!" This is why every Christian cannot help but be an evangelist, spreading everywhere the good news of the faith. It is as if I were on my deathbed dying of cancer and someone suddenly came to me announcing that the cure had just been found. This is why the early Christians proclaimed the Resurrection of Jesus with such rejoicing and unrestrained enthusiasm. Christ is risen and our sins are forgiven! Christ is risen and death is overcome! Christ is risen to fill us with the power of the Holy Spirit! Christ is risen and with him we too rise to a life that is life indeed!" "In the world you have tribulation, but rejoice, I have overcome the world," said Jesus.

How often we hear it said of a person, "Boy, is he bad news!" Of Christ it may be said unequivocally that he is the best news ever to hit this planet. We Christians, as followers of Christ, may best be described as God's 'good news people.' As carriers of God's good news, we are sustained by unending hope. Suffering and defeat are known, but never accepted as final; new beginnings are always possible. Energized by the Holy Spirit who makes all things new, we light candles rather than curse the darkness; and we express in our living the fruit of the Spirit: "love, joy, peace, patience, goodness, faithfulness, gentleness, self-control" (Gal 5.22-23).

This is the good news we are called to preach—good news about God's love, good news about God's forgiveness, good news about God's power for our weakness, good news about the death of death in Christ's Resurrection, good news about our Great liberator, the Lord Jesus! It is no wonder that Saint Gregory of Nyssa speaks of the preaching of the Gospel as a "liberator from tyranny."

This is why every Christian preacher is best described as an evangelist: a bearer of good news! In view of this, one wonders how people can attend some churches for years without hearing the good news!

Saint Paul describes this good news with words such as "unsearchable riches" and "unspeakable gifts" and "We have this treasure." And he feels driven to share it: "Necessity is laid upon me; woe is me if I preach not the Gospel!"

D. T. Niles describes the evangelist as a "beggar": "Evangelism is one beggar telling another beggar where to get food. The Christian does not offer out of his own bounty. He has no bounty. He is simply a guest at his Master's table, and, as an evangelist, he calls others too."

The task of the preacher may at times require him to warn, to speak of God's judgment; but basically, and beyond all else, it will be a message of good news, the message of God's insane love for each one of us which drove him to offer his own Son for our salvation.

Dorothy Sayer said once, "You have the greatest good news on earth—the Incarnation of God in human life—and you treat it as an insignificant news item fit for page fourteen in the chronicle of daily events."

We can turn on T.V. and get the news, but it is not redemptive. If our preaching is anything, the one thing it must be is redemptive. It must be like a candle burning in a dark night, or a drink of fresh water in a parched desert. "Do the work of an evangelist," Paul writes to Timothy (2 Tim 4.5).

Christopher Morley was observing the telephone one day and he began to think of the people who were waiting somewhere to hear some good news: parents waiting to hear from a child far from home, a lonely shut-in waiting to hear from a friend, the unemployed waiting to receive a job offer. He said that suddenly he wished he could call them all and give each of them some good news. Is not this what we have been ordained to do? The good news we preach is headline stuff. It is not going door to door selling some remedies; rather, it is the standing on the street corner yelling, "Extra!" It is the greatest good news this world has ever heard or will ever hear!

3
Preparing the Sermon

As if I had to entertain a demanding audience that could not tolerate any poor performance. No wonder that this attitude leads to fatigue and eventually to exhaustion...The question is not 'Do I have time to prepare?', but 'Do I live in a state of preparedness?' When God is my only concern...the center of my interest, when all my prayers, reading, studying, speaking and writing serve only to know God better and to make him known better, then there is no basis for anxiety or stage fright. Then I can live in such a state of preparedness and trust that speaking from the heart is also speaking to the heart.[31]

A young author asked Stephen Leacock what tricks of the trade he employed when he sat down to write. "No tricks," said the humorist. "I seat myself at my desk, wait until an idea occurs and then jot it down." "You make writing seem so simple," said the young author. "Writing is simple," replied Leacock. "It's the occurring that's difficult."

It is indeed the 'occurring' that is difficult. It is difficult because, for the most part, it does not 'occur.' One has to

---

[31] Henri Nouwen, *The Genesee Diary* (Garden City, N.Y., 1981).

study, and read, and pray and work for it to occur. One of the great American preachers, Harry Emerson Fosdick, said once that you drench the congregation in your life's blood every time you preach. Long ago in ancient Greece a wise man said, "The gates of excellence are surrounded by a sea of sweat." A preacher once scoffed at the efforts of another preacher and said, "Why, he's all broken out in a sweat when he finishes his sermon!" Well, God help the preacher who works up a sweat mowing the lawn, or playing golf, but not ever preaching a sermon. For what is more worthy of sweat than the Gospel?

Consider some of the things of lesser importance in life for which people are willing to sweat.

Have you ever paused to consider how many hours, days and weeks advertising people literally sweat it out in order to prepare a thirty-second commercial for the mass media in order to sell orange juice? Newscasters work an entire day to prepare each day's newscasts.

Ben Hogan would prepare for a golf tournament weeks in advance. He would first go out and study the course meticulously. He would practice for hours until his hands were blistered and raw. Then he would take a club to his hotel room and practice at night. Every shot with which he was confronted in competition he had made one hundred times before.

Vince Lombardi, the great football coach, once told his players, "Practice doesn't make perfect; perfect practice makes perfect." A 'National Football League Coach of the Year,' who was a former student of Lombardi, said of him,

"The world's full of mediocre people. Coach Lombardi taught me that you can rise above that with hard work."

The popular notion that Abraham Lincoln wrote his most famous speech on the back of an envelope while en route by train to Gettysburg is false. Lincoln started work on the first draft well before the event. He wrote, re-wrote, fussed over it; and the draft he delivered was written on the kind of paper Lincoln regularly used in the White House.

I once asked the famous pianist, Gina Bachauer, how often she practiced. She replied that she practiced many hours each day well into the night. In fact, when her fingers blistered and bled from too much practice, she would bandage them and resume practicing.

One would not believe the amount of practice and preparation that goes into a TV talk show like Johnny Carson. The questions and answers are reviewed and rehearsed in advance. No deviation from the script is allowed except on Johnny Carson's part (with ad libs prepared by his writers). If a guest deviates from the script, Johnny will politely excuse himself and say something like, "And now here's Ed with good news for hungry dogs."

Think of Demosthenes and the stutter he had to sweat over for hours each day. For years down at the sea he practiced speaking with pebbles in his mouth until he finally overcame it. He became one of the greatest of all orators.

When a preacher saw the ceiling of the famous Sistine Chapel, he thought to himself: if painting that ceiling was worth a life of total dedication and devotion on the part of Michaelangelo, is not our task of painting a picture of God with words—a picture that will inspire and change the lives of God's children—is not that worth far more consecration?

A noted preacher was asked how long it took him to prepare one of his sermons. He replied, "All my life." "How long does it take to prepare a sermon?" is a rather ambiguous question. If you mean how long it takes to write a manuscript, then a day may be enough; but if you mean how long it takes to think through a sermon, then it may be ten, twenty or thirty years. I personally have been collecting material on some sermons for over thirty years.

We live in a society where the word 'self-discipline' has become a lost word. The preacher must be careful lest he lose the treasures that only self-discipline can yield. The only way to prepare sermons worthy of our Lord is to work hard. Preaching that costs nothing accomplishes nothing. As the famous American preacher, John Jowett, said, "If the study is a lounge, the pulpit will be an impertinence. It is, therefore, imperative that the preacher go into his study to do hard work."

Good preaching has never been easy. Those who find it easy simply aren't good preachers. Chrysostom worked hard and came into the pulpit well prepared, as we can see when we read his inspiring homilies.

In Irving Stone's biographical novel, *The Agony and the Ecstasy*, Bertoldo, the master sculptor, speaks to the young, aspiring Michaelangelo. "Dedication is expensive," he says. "It will cost you your life." Michaelangelo, with great insight, replies, "What else is life for?" If this is true for the sculptor, is it not even more true of the preacher?

Good preaching may look easy; it may appear spontaneous and effortless, but there will be hours of preparation
behind it. There are those who despise preparation, claim-
ing that it is all too human and nullifies their dependence
on the Holy Spirit for inspiration. But when one person
heard one of these preachers who never prepared but left
everything to the Holy Spirit, he said of his sermon, "I
never knew that the Holy Spirit could be so dull and un-
interesting." We do not say that there is not room for the
Holy Spirit in our preaching. He is the one who is behind
all faithful preaching of the word of God. But the better
prepared a preacher is, the more effectively the Holy Spirit
can use him.

Very often priests who are not great orators have a high
opinion of their preaching. One such priest had preached
at the evening service when an archbishop was present.
Afterwards, the priest said to His Eminence, "I pledged
myself always to preach extemporaneously in the evening." Lifting up his hands, the archbishop said quietly,
"Kneel down and I'll absolve you of the pledge."

People are not tired of good preaching. They are tired
of bad preaching, preaching that is non-preaching, irrele-
vant preaching, uninspired preaching, insipid preaching,
unprepared preaching.

A famous preacher tells of meeting Christ as he was
mounting the pulpit with manuscript in hand. Looking at
the sermon in his hands, Jesus said, "Is this the best you
could do for me?" I think all of us need to meet Christ not
only as we mount the pulpit, but also in our study each
day. We need to have him confront us regularly with that
same question: "Is this the best you could do for me?"

Here I recall the Prophet Samuel's response in the Old Testament. It should become our prayer as we prepare for Sunday's sermon: "I will not offer burnt offerings to the Lord my God which cost me nothing" (2 Sam 24.24).

Much has been written about the fragmentation of the pastor. He seems to be busy doing everything but that for which he was specifically prepared and ordained: to preach the word and administer the sacraments. The average priest's name today is 'legion.' He tries to be a legion of things to people: administrator, counselor, social worker, educator, pastor, custodian, secretary, mimeographer, plumber, carpenter, husband and father. If he truly tries to fulfill all these roles, he will end up with a breakdown. He needs to establish some real priorities. He needs to say, "This one thing I do. For this one thing I have been prepared and called. It is to this I will give the best of my time and effort." We must remember what the apostles did when their role was about to be fragmented. They said, "It is not right that we should give up preaching the word of God to serve tables. Therefore, brethren, pick out from among you seven men of good repute, full of the Spirit and wisdom, whom we may appoint to this duty. But we will devote ourselves to prayer and to the ministry of the word" (Acts 6.2-4).

James S. Stewart, perhaps the greatest contemporary preacher, said in the Warrack Lectures of 1955:

> It is because the message entrusted to us is of such paramount importance that we should labor at it day and night, sparing no pains to become skilled in our craft and to make the earthen vessel as worthy as we can of the treasure it contains.

Finding the Time

An admirer of Marian Anderson, the famous opera singer, once remarked to her: "I'd give my right arm if I could sing like you." Miss Anderson smiled and replied thoughtfully, "Would you give eight hours of practice a day?"

One of the secrets of good preaching is the amount of time we are willing to dedicate to it. One must learn to spend three or four mornings a week at a place where one can be reached only in case of emergency and where one can do nothing but study, pray and write. The priest who will resolutely keep his morning hours segregated from invasion will find his whole ministry enriched, deepened and energized. I have chosen the morning hours in my ministry because they are the clearest and freest hours. My mind is clearest after a good night's sleep. The mornings are also more free since they are unencumbered by parish meetings and family responsibilities as are the evenings. Since I am an early riser, I am up at six or before and spend three or four hours in study four or five mornings a week in a secluded study in my home. There are no interruptions during these morning hours, and one can spend the time not only for sermon preparation, but also for one's own spiritual growth and nourishment. The discipline of reserving certain hours each day for the preparation of yourself and your message will impose an excellent order on your schedule and will help establish a real priority in your daily life.

Efficiency experts, now called time management counselors, tell us that people have more energy in the morning and can do more things more effectively in the morning. Thus, the important things—the 'A' jobs—are done in the morning. The less important 'C' jobs are saved for low energy times. The 'A' job for every preacher is to be in contact with God and his saints in study and prayer. This all-important 'A' job is reserved for the best part of the day when clarity of mind and energy are at their highest and best—the morning. We are reminded that Jesus "in the morning, a great while before day...rose and went out to a lonely place...and prayed" (Mk 1.25).

Time for Prayer

A good sermon is born out of an intimate, prayerful dialogue with God on the scriptural text to be preached on. "You preach as if you had come straight from the Presence," someone said to a great preacher. He replied, "I did."

The weakness of preaching has its source in the poverty of the average pastor's spirituality. He finds little or no time for prayer. Preaching comes out of the preacher's relationship with God, and his preaching reflects this relationship. To communicate the Gospel, those who do it have to be on fire and that means they must be people of prayer. One must so bathe himself and his message in prayer that the actual delivery of the sermon is praise to God; and when at last it is time for closing, the concluding prayer will flow naturally out of the preaching. I believe firmly that since every sermon is conceived in prayer, born in prayer, grows in prayer and is delivered in prayer, it is only natural that it conclude in prayer. A sermon that does not conclude with prayer leaves something unfinished.

We cannot say too much about the importance of prayer in the ministry of preaching. There is a legendary story of a preacher who was marvelously used by God. He dreamed one night that he was beginning to take pride in himself and his gifts. But an angel told him that his success was due primarily to a poor widow who sat regularly at the foot of his pulpit and never ceased to pray for him.

Saint Symeon the New Theologian brought together the two main lines of authentic Orthodox Christian spirituality: the intellectual school of the Alexandrians (Clement and the Cappadocians) and that of the so-called 'affective' school of the heart (John Klimakos, Nilos, et. al.). The true theologians, according to Symeon, were *theodidaktoi*, literally 'taught by God' through prayer and the Holy Spirit. Every preacher is called to be *theodidaktos*, taught by God, within the realm of the Sacred Tradition of the Church, of course.

There is a sort of intellectualism in the churches of the West that has infected the East. The main criterion for admission to the pulpit is a university degree. But we need to remember that in the East for many centuries the main criterion for admission to the pulpit was not a university degree, but a period of extended training in a monastery where theological training was combined with a life of prayer and worship. The preachers of the East traditionally have come out of a life of prayer. They were trained and called to be *theodidaktoi*.

As *theodidaktos*, the preacher realizes that his message is not his own; it is given to him by the Holy Spirit. He preaches not his own view or opinions, but the truth of God. He searches and studies; but having studied, searched and learned, he must then wait for the voice and guidance of the Spirit to come to him.

Fr. Alexander Schmemann writes in his book For the Life of the World:

> The early Christians realized that in order to be-
> come of the Holy Spirit, they must ascend to heaven
> where Christ has ascended. They realized also that
> this ascension was the very condition of their mis-
> sion in the world, of their ministry to the world. For
> there—in heaven—they were immersed in the new
> life of the kingdom; and when after this 'liturgy of the
> ascension' they returned into the world, their very
> faces reflected the light, the joy and peace of that
> kingdom, and they were truly its witnesses. They
> brought no programs and no theories; but wherever
> they went, the seeds of the kingdom sprouted, faith
> was kindled, life was transfigured, things impossible
> were made possible. They were witnesses; and when
> they were asked, 'Whence shines this light, where is
> the source of this power?', they knew what to answer
> and where to lead men.[32]

If our ministry of preaching is to be effective, we must find time to ascend daily through prayer to where Christ is. This is the necessary pre-condition of our ministry in the world and for the world. It is not enough that our mind be filled with ideas about God. Our heart must also dwell with him. For true prayer is "to descend with the mind into the heart, and there to stand before the face of the Lord, ever-present, all-seeing, within you" (Theophan the Recluse). According to Orthodox spirituality, the way to

---

[32]   Schmemann, For the Life of the World. (Crestwood, N.Y.).

God is not primarily through the mind, but through the heart. It is when we enter into the heart with the mind that we discover the kingdom of God. As Saint Isaak the Syrian writes, "Try to enter the treasure chamber...that is within you and then you will discover the treasure chamber of heaven. For they are one and the same. If you succeed in entering one, you will see both. The ladder to this kingdom is hidden inside you, in your soul. If you wish your soul clean of sin, you will see there the rungs of the ladder which you may climb." John Karpathios says, "It takes great effort and struggle in prayer to reach that state of mind which is free from all disturbance; it is heaven within the heart, the place, as the Apostle Paul assures us, 'where Christ dwells in us' (2 Cor 13.5)." It is out of this personal and intimate encounter with Jesus that our preaching is born. Saint John so well expressed it when he wrote, "That which...we have heard, which we have seen with our own eyes, which we have looked upon and touched with our hands, concerning the word of life   This is the message we have heard from him and proclaim to you..." (1 Jn 1.1, 5).

Thus, the daily period of prayer and study, especially during the quiet early morning hours, is for the preacher the sine qua non of his ministry. Each priest is called to fashion his own 'monastery' and 'desert' and to retreat there daily for wisdom and strength. Henri Nouwen writes:

> We have, indeed, to fashion our own desert where we can withdraw every day, shake off our compulsions, and dwell in the gentle healing presence of our Lord. Without such a desert we will lose our own

soul while preaching the Gospel to others. But with such a spiritual abode, we will become increasingly conformed to him in whose name we minister. The very first thing we need to do is set apart a time and place to be with God and him alone.... Solitude is thus the place of purification, the place of the great struggle and the great encounter. Solitude is not simply a means to an end. Solitude is its own end. It is the place where Christ remodels us in his own image and frees us from the victimizing compulsions of the world. Solitude is the place of our salvation...Saint Anthony spent twenty years in isolation. When he left it, he took his solitude with him and shared it with all who came to him. Those who saw him described him as balanced, gentle, and caring. He had become so Christlike, so radiant with God's love, that his entire being was ministry.[33]

An important aspect of the priest's prayer life will be daily repentance and confession to God. Jesus said, "Blessed are the pure in heart, for they shall see God." No one can see God or know God without purity of heart. In the words of Saint John of the Ladder, "Purity... is the foundation of theology— Purity makes its disciple a theologian, who of himself grasps the dogmas of the Trinity."[34] Purity of heart sees God, and anything that besmirches the purity spoils the vision. One of the prime pre-conditions of good preaching is daily contrition, sorrow, repentance and confession in the life of the preacher.

When Arsenios prayed, "Lord, lead me in the way of salvation," he heard a voice saying, "Arsenios, flee, be silent

---

[33]   Nouwen, Henri, *The Way of the Heart* (New York, 1981).

[34]   *The Ladder of Divine Ascent* (London, 1959).

and pray always, for these are the sources of sinlessness."
As preachers we, too, need to heed those words: 'flee,' 'be
silent' and 'pray always.' We must flee daily into the desert we have fashioned for ourselves, there to be silent before God and listen before we speak in his behalf, and to
pray for every word we preach. If our preaching is to be
a word of power, it must come out of silence and prayer.
This explains the weight of Moses' personality when he
came down from the mountain, and Jesus' after a period
of prayer, and Paul's, whose ministry began only after he
had spent years in the desert where he was taught by God.

The best sermon is preached by the priest who has a
sermon to preach, not by the one who has to preach a
sermon. No priest will ever have a sermon to preach if
he does not flee to his desert regularly to make time for
silence and prayer, to let God speak to him. Evagrios of
Pontos said, "He who prays, truly is a theologian; and he is
a theologian who prays truly." I should like to paraphrase
this important statement as follows: "He who prays, truly
knows God; and he is the one who knows God who truly
prays." How can any preacher have anything to say about
God without prayer?

We must be careful that the inner fire, the flame of the
Holy Spirit burning in our soul, is fed regularly so that it
will be burning constantly to give warmth and light to the
lost travelers whom we shall be meeting out in that cold
world not only on Sundays, but throughout the week as
we minister for Christ.

Jesus did not begin his public preaching ministry until he was anointed by the Holy Spirit on Epiphany. The
apostles did not preach until the Spirit came upon them

at Pentecost. Both these events have much to teach us in our preaching ministry. The dynamic of great preaching has always been the dynamic of the Holy Spirit within us. If there is a decline in preaching today, it is due more than anything else to the fact that the Holy Spirit is ignored as the supreme inspirer of preaching. I have never undertaken to preach a sermon without declaring myself to be an empty vessel and asking humbly to be filled with the wisdom and guidance of the Holy Spirit. As a result, I can never know which part of the message is mine and which is of the Holy Spirit.

I must mention here that if the Orthodox priest is to grow spiritually, he should strive to find a spiritual elder (*pneumatikos pateras*) in order to keep evaluating his total ministry. Self- evaluation is a difficult and dangerous thing. One priest asked once, "Why can't I see any spiritual growth in my life? Everybody else tells me they can see it." He was reminded that at Pentecost no man could see the flame over his own head, but he could see what was burning over his brother's head. I suppose this is something that should keep us very humble. Yet if we are to progress, we do need someone to help us evaluate our ministry objectively.

A teacher of homiletics said once, "Prepare your sermon as if there were no Holy Spirit, but then deliver it with the conviction that there is." I suppose he was trying to prevent his students from ceasing to read and study because they were relying so much on the Holy Spirit to guide them. Personally, I prefer to prepare and deliver my sermons with the conviction that there is a Holy Spirit both before, during, and after the sermon. I depend on the Holy Spirit to guide me in my reading and studying, to create order out of the chaos of notes and thoughts I accumulate before each sermon. I depend on him to help select a topic that will speak to the real needs of God's people, to take every thought and make it captive to Christ. It has been said that preaching, like genius, is 99% perspiration and 1% inspiration. My experience has taught me that even the perspiration, together with the love that is behind it, is a gift of the Holy Spirit. Every sermon I prepare begins with an epiklesis prayer to the Holy Spirit that he transubstantiate my thoughts and words into living words of everlasting life for God's people.

I like these words by Bishop Ignatios of Latakia:

> Without the Holy Spirit, God is far away,
> Christ stays in the past, the Gospel is a dead letter.
> The Church is simply an organization, prayer is
> merely a formality, the Liturgy an empty ritual,
> Christian living a slave morality.
> But with the Holy Spirit all changes:
> the cosmos is resurrected, it groans with the
> birthpangs of the kingdom.
> The risen Christ is here,
> life is pervaded by joy and praise,
> the Gospel becomes a living letter from Christ,
> our human acts are done in Christ and for Christ.

Know Those to Whom You Preach

A priest's sermon concerned the relationship between fact and faith. "That you are sitting before me in this church," he said, "is fact. That I am standing here speaking from this pulpit is fact. But it is only faith that makes me believe anyone is listening."

Many are not listening. There are many reasons for this. Many sermons are simply not hitting the target. They seem to be aimed two or three miles above where most people really live. "Our pastor is always scratching us where we don't itch," said one parishioner. If preaching is dull, it is because it does not connect with the real needs of people.

It is not enough to know the Gospel we are called to preach. We must also know the people to whom we bring the Gospel. Jesus intimated this when he gave us the parable of the soils. Just as the farmer needs to know the kind of soil with which he is working, so the pastor needs to know the problems and the anxieties of his flock. This is the soil into which he will sow the seed of the word of God. The kind of seed he sows must be suited to the particular soil. Each week in our preaching a special verse will be chosen from the lectionary that applies to some specific problems and needs of the people in the congregation. When this is done competently, it assures that our preaching will not drift off into abstractions, but will remain in touch with the lives of real people. There are two books every preacher must know well: the Bible and the book of the human heart. Lord Chesterfield said once, "Learning is acquired by reading books, but the much more necessary learning, the knowledge of the world, is only to be acquired by reading men and studying all the various editions of them." We do not select a passage or topic for the sermon because it fascinates us. We select it because we know that it relates directly to the needs, interests, problems and concerns of our people. A few years ago Mr. Silverman, a genius in TV programming, started at CBS, went to ABC, then became president of NBC. He was one of the most sought after men in the industry. The reason for this was that he knew what people wanted to see on television, and he addressed himself to what the people out there really wanted. Every preacher is called to do the same: to take the needs of the people in one hand and the truth of the Gospel in the other and bring the two together in the sermon.

This is the way Jesus preached. "As he landed he saw a great throng, and he had compassion on them, because they were like sheep without a shepherd; and he began to teach them many things" (Mk 6.34). Jesus' message grew out of his knowledge of the needs of his people.

Fant and Pinson in *Twenty Centuries of Great Preaching* come to the conclusion that "great preaching is relevant preaching." By relevant preaching they mean preaching that meets the needs of the people where they are living, preaching that comes from one who truly cares and wants to help.

It takes a lifetime of living with people to come to know their needs. This is perhaps the reason an Orthodox consultation on preaching stated that "the Orthodox priest is ordained in and married to a particular parish with the implication that this relationship is for life. We do realize that 'by economy' (*kat' oikonomia*) the Church, in certain circumstances, has allowed for the movement and transfer of local pastors, but we must insist that this 'theme' of marriage to a particular parish is vital in the sense that there must be a deep intimacy and caring for the entire life of the people of God on the part of that priest."[35]

The word we preach is not just proclaimed, it is also addressed—personally addressed to each person in the congregation. It is not marked 'Occupant' or 'To whom it may concern.' It has a specific name on it. Let me use an example. A few years ago I was traveling in the Middle East and it was difficult for mail to catch up with me. At the same time I was writing and sending letters back home. Because my wife's mail had not reached me, my letters rarely reflected any knowledge of the experiences at home. I rarely answered any questions which she had asked. So it is with good preaching. It must be in real contact with the questions and needs of the people and must address itself constantly to those needs. The shepherd must know his sheep, and the sheep the shepherd.

The big question is how? How does a shepherd get to know his sheep well enough so that he will be addressing his messages to specific people with specific needs and not to everyone in general and no one in particular?

We come,to know our people well through parish visitation. It is only by visiting with our people and listening to them that we discover the heresies that need to be addressed in our preaching, the troubles that they're facing each day. I know that parish visitation is not as fashionable as it once was, and I think this is disastrous for preach-

---

[35]   "Orthodox Consultation on Preaching and Teaching the Christian Faith Today," St. Vladimir's Theological Quarterly 25, n.2 (1981).

ing. If we don't know our people, how can we address the Gospel to them in a living, dynamic way? The pastor who walks close to his people during the week and knows their daily problems will have no difficulty communicating well with the listener in the pew.

Many important things cannot be learned in books. Only by going out among people, listening to their problems and sharing their troubles can we be prepared to speak to them in a dynamic way. The advice a novelist once gave to a young writer is good advice for every preacher, "Do not rack your brain contriving plots. Get out among the people. See them, hear them, study them." Know your congregation, their needs, their problems, their aspirations, their sins and their heresies. Keep ever in touch with those needs and your sermons will be on target.

Some of the means that can be used to get to know our people, in addition to parish visitation, are personal counseling, the sacrament of penance, questionnaires on basic attitudes, beliefs and values, small Bible study groups and a specific discussion group that will focus on the pastor's sermon. This will be discussed a little later in this book.

It has been said that the hospital diagnoses before it prescribes; the Church prescribes before it diagnoses. It is easy to become defensive and say that the Church has a divine prescription, as well as a divine diagnosis. That may be true, yet the souls of men are so delicate and complex that their spiritual needs will not be met by mass prescriptions.

Let us take the synoptic Gospels as an example. If we line up Mark, Matthew and Luke in parallel columns, we note that there are many similarities; indeed, they can be looked at together (*syn*—together; *optic*—look at) and read together. This is why they are called synoptic Gospels. Yet, similar as they are, the three synoptic Gospels differ slightly because they were written by different people writing at different times and in different places. They present varying emphases because they were addressed to different audiences. Each Gospel is tailored to the needs of a specific community of people. It is the same Gospel, but its presentation is adapted to suit the religious needs of a specific audience. Each of the Gospel writers knew well the needs of his audience. The same Gospel is adapted to suit those needs.

To know our people is to know where they hurt, where they falter, where they need shoring up and, indeed, where they need to be reminded of God's judgment, as well as his grace. In discussing what makes a drama great, the playwright Arthur Miller said that in any successful play there must be something which makes the audience say within themselves, "My God, that's me!" The same can be said for preaching. And that must come out of the involvement of the preacher in the life of his people.

How well the following poem summarizes the need for the preacher to climb down from the pulpit to be with his people:

The Preacher's Mistake

The parish priest
Of Austerity,
Climbed up in a high church steeple
To be nearer God,

So that he might hand
His word down to His people.
And in sermon script He daily wrote
What he thought was sent from heaven,
And he dropped this down
On his people's heads Two times one day in seven.
In his age God said,
"Come down and die!"
And he cried from the steeple,
"Where art Thou, Lord?"
And the Lord replied,
"Down here among my people."

Brewer Mattocks

A second way to try to understand the needs of the people to whom we preach is to try the following experiment. Try sitting in a different pew each day during the week as you pray. Try to visualize the person who sat in that pew the past Sunday. Ask yourself questions such as: "What did I say to the person who sat in this pew last Sunday? Did I speak to his real needs? Did I say anything to help him or did I speak over his head? How about my sermon for next Sunday? Will it hold his attention? Will it speak to this person's real needs?"

Remember Ezekiel in the Old Testament? He was about to speak bitterly to the captives by the river. But God said to him, "No, Ezekiel, not yet. Sit down." And Ezekiel sat down. "For seven days I sat where they sat," he said. For seven days Ezekiel listened to the people, entered into their problems and pains. For seven days he learned sympathy and understanding by sitting where they sat. Then God said to him, "Now you may speak." And when he spoke it was with great sympathy and understanding. He addressed real problems, real pains and real temptations. Every preacher needs to sit where his people sit before he speaks.

If we truly sit where our people sit, we shall realize that we are dealing for the most part with broken hearts, broken dreams, broken plans and broken lives. And if we preach to broken hearts, we shall seldom miss the mark. Both Ann Landers and Dear Abby write for 1,000 newspapers with 13,000,000 readers. Dear Abby gets 25,000 letters a week. To get an idea of what people are burdened about, every preacher should read their columns.

A pastor looked out upon his congregation one Sunday morning. This is what he saw in that cross section of humanity. On the back pew sat a boy who had accidentally broken a neighbor's window and sought strength to confess it. In a front pew sat an elderly woman who lost her husband last week and sought comfort for her grief. In another pew sat a youth burdened with guilt because last night, in a moment of passion, he had violated his moral principles. In still another pew sat a couple worshiping in gratitude for their son who had just graduated from college and found an excellent job. In a back pew sat a middle-aged woman who had drifted so deeply into sin that she was contemplating suicide. On the other side sat a couple, married for twenty years, who were on the verge of divorce, and no one around them even suspected their difficulty.

These are some of the burdens people come to church with every Sunday. They are problems that should be addressed if our preaching is to be vital. On any given Sunday people will be waiting to listen through ears of hearts that have been pierced and broken, people who are discouraged, depressed and despairing. They need to hear some good word from God's servant that might set their lives free, that might lift some load and give them reason to dream again, hope again and walk again. This is why whenever we preach, we must always try to preach to broken hearts because we can safely assume that there is at least one in every pew.

Another way for the preacher to come to know the real needs of his people is by praying for them each day. A good way to do this is by keeping the parish directory in the altar area and slipping in for a few moments each day for prayer. During this prayer time, the priest may open the directory and pray by name for two or three families each day. As he prays in this manner, he will visualize their work, difficulties and temptations. God will no doubt remind him of certain needs in each family that the pastor may have forgotten and how these needs may be met. In any instance, a preacher who follows this plan regularly will come away with a far greater knowledge and understanding of the real needs of his people.

Another pastor begins his preaching by setting down on paper the initials of a dozen or more people whom he has met or seen during the past week. Opposite each initial he places a sentence summary of the need of that person. Then he says to himself, "This is a cross section of next Sunday's congregation. These are the souls to which I must bring the Gospel. Unless my sermon speaks to their condition, it will not be a sermon." In summary, then, we must always strive to keep in our mind's eye the real needs of the people to whom we shall be speaking. These needs can best be understood through parish visitation, personal counseling, contact in small Bible study and discussion groups, questionnaires, by sitting where our people sit, by keeping specific persons and needs in mind when we preach and by making sure our preaching has something hopeful and healing to say to the many broken hearts that are in every congregation. Since the preacher, too, is human, he is not one who stands apart from the needs of his people. He understands since he himself has the same needs. One preacher used to say that he would preach to himself and then find out that he had preached to all other people.

Finally, if we are to really know the needs of our people, we must realize that there will be those who will resist and oppose our efforts to bring the Gospel to them. This will often discourage some of us and produce in us a very depressing what's-the-use attitude that can be very destructive to our ministry. Jesus encountered such people. Who are we to expect that we shall be spared? Dr. Paul Tillich addressed this topic in his address to graduating students at Union Theological Seminary on 24 May 1955. Speaking on the verse, "Heal the sick; cast out demons" (Mt 10:8), this is what he said in part:

> Members of the outgoing class, friends! The first difficulty you will experience when Jesus sends you ahead of him and gives you the power of healing is many people will tell you that they do not need healing. And if you come to them with the claim that you will cast out the demons which rule their lives, they

will laugh at you and tell you that you have a demon, just as they said to Jesus.

Therefore, the first task of a minister is to make men aware of their predicament. Many of those who went out from our seminary to congregations and communities became despaired about this task... They forgot more and more that their task is to heal those who are sick, including those who are not aware that they are sick. There is no easy way of making them aware of their predicament. God, certainly, has his ways to do so. He shakes the complacency of those who consider themselves to be healthy by throwing them into darkness and despair, externally or internally. He reveals to them what they are by undercutting the foundations of their self-assurance. He reveals their blindness about themselves. We cannot do this, not even with ourselves. But we can be open for the moment in which it happens. And if it happens we can become tools of the power which may heal them.

Know God's Word

Preparation for good preaching includes a lifelong study of God's word in Scripture. We are literally to 'eat' the scroll of God's word and digest it so that it becomes part of our being as the angel ordered in Saint John's vision (Rev 10.8-9). We are to dwell in the word, memorizing it, praying it, enjoying it, coming back to it again and again, chewing on it as a cow chews her cud. The word of God is to become for us the other food' of which Jesus spoke. "I have food to eat of which you do not know" (Jn 3:32). We are to read the Scriptures daily not just for sermon preparation, but also for personal growth and the sheer enjoyment of God's word. One of the greatest contemporary preachers, Archbishop Fulton Sheen, said, "Try spending one hour a day meditating upon the Scriptures and see how soon you'll become a preacher of God's word." A good plan for the preacher to follow is to read four chapters each day from Scripture, one each from the Gospels, the Epistles, the Psalms and one from the Old Testament books.

In selecting a text for preaching, it is important to re-member the words of William Barclay, "He who chooses a great text is half way on the road to producing a good sermon." Once the text is selected one must, in the words of Bengal, "Apply yourself totally to the text; apply the text totally to yourself." We are told of Saint Chrysostom that he "works steadily through the chosen passage; he tries to let it speak to himself and hopes that in this way it will speak to his hearers. He often appears to wander, but in reality he never loses sight of the main theme that he has in hand. The sermon is a real exposition of the word of God, and often the sharp and piercing word will find its target in the hearts of the hearers."[36] What is true of some sermons today, which begin with a Scripture text only to wander completely away from it so that the body of the sermon bears no relationship to the text, was not true of Chrysostom. Someone said of this type of preaching: "If the Scripture text had the measles, the sermon would not have caught it."

It is important to let the Scripture speak to us first; for this reason we should not consult commentaries first,

---

[36]   Stephen Neill, *Chrysostom and His Message* (New York, 1962).

but let the text speak to us personally and existentially in prayer. Fr. William Skudlarek, O.S.B., writes:

> Do everything you can to stay close to the texts. Read them aloud, check different translations, work on the original. But stay with the texts. Do not, at this point in the process of preparation, go to the commentaries or to any of the multitude of homiletic aids. You will be tempted to do this, especially if you find something that is particularly difficult or troubling in a text. But trust in your own ability to hear and understand. Don't let someone else tell you what the text means. The text is speaking to you, to you as an individual and to you as a representative of the community. Only you can hear what it is saying, here and now. Don't be worried that you are going to make some foolish error in interpretation. You stand within a living tradition, and from this tradition you have inherited a way of approaching the Scriptures that is so much a part of you that you may not even recognize it. Furthermore, your formal studies in the field of Scripture and theology are a safeguard against error. Finally, the Church's willingness to authorize you as a preacher is a clear sign that, because of character and training, you are judged to be responsible in your handling of the Scriptures. So stay with the difficult text, struggle with it, pray with it, chew on it. Speak to it and let it speak to you. Sometime in the middle of the week the time comes for checking the commentaries...From midweek until Friday is the...time for letting go, for allowing the process of incubation to take place
>
> And then comes Friday, when you...should set aside a couple of hours to work on the homily... it took

me years to discover that I had to block out time for myself if I was to have it.[37]

If our sermon is based on God's word, one liturgical gesture that should cease is the closing of the Gospel book following the reading of the Gospel lesson. If the sermon or homily proceeds from the Gospel lesson just read; the book should remain open during the sermon to show that the words we speak proceed from it. They are God's words, not ours. If the sermon text is to be read, it should be read directly from the open Gospel book. If additional verses are cited during the homily, they should be cited from the already open Gospel book. The open Gospel book will serve as a forceful reminder that the homily is, in reality, God speaking his word to us through his inspired book.

Prepare by Reading

The demands made on the pastor's time are enormous. In addition, he is expected to continue his professional growth by attending all kinds of conferences, retreats and seminars. But year in and year out there is no more effective instrument for the pastor's growth than books. And what can be more accessible than books?

Abraham Lincoln's schooling was negligible, the aggregate, he said, not amounting to one year. Yet he was one of the most well-read, thoughtful and insightful presidents we have had. The secret was that he read almost constantly.

In Belva Plain's novel *Evergreen* the story is told of a sixteen-year-old Polish immigrant youth coming to the United States with an immense thirst for knowledge, yet

---

[37]   Skudlarek, *The Word.*

unable to attend school because of poverty and long work hours in the sweatshops of New York. A friend, who happened to be a teacher, told him, "Don't be discouraged that you cannot attend school. You can learn as much or more by reading, reading, reading and reading."

A young person who was eager to preach even though he had not finished school said, "I believe that God will fill my mouth." His father replied, "Yes, God will fill your mouth if you fill your head first."

Ruth said to Naomi in the Old Testament, "I went out full and I came back empty." That is the plight of the preacher. He goes out to the pulpit full and he comes back empty. He must find a way to keep himself full. The fullness comes through the Holy Spirit who works through our prayer life, but also through our reading. One preacher says, "I have insomnia so I read at night. I read almost everything with a sense of 'How does this relate to my preaching?' " The famous American preacher John Henry Jowett wrote, "Enter your study at an appointed hour and let that hour be as early as the earliest of your businessmen who goes to his warehouse or his office."

A study of the habits of great preachers reports that all of them had been eager students possessed with an insatiable desire to read and gather information.[38]

A personal examination of the study habits of great American preachers revealed the following. One spent twelve hours a day in his study. Another spent thirty hours on each sermon. Still another spent an hour of preparation

---

[38]   D.E. Demaray, *Pulpit Giants* (Chicago, 1973).

for each minute he preached. Some rabbis, I am told, go home and read all afternoon.

The average parish preacher today gives very little time to the preparation of sermons. Preparation is usually left to the end of the week when other parish duties have been completed. The result is that the average preacher hardly reads more than one serious book a year. It has been said that the so-called 'Saturday-night thumb' comes from spending most Saturday nights thumbing through books of sermons, collections of snappy sermon illustrations and other sources of 'heat-and-serve' sermons. The emotional concomitant to this thumb disease is called the 'nothing-to-preach jitters.' It is a terrible disease. Fortunately, the prognosis for therapy is good, as we shall soon see.

A young priest said after finishing his first year of preaching in a parish, "I've preached through all the ideas and research I had done for term papers, class essays and student sermons. Now I am preached out. What should I do?"

The answer to that question is, "Read! Read! Read!" You will never run out of material and ideas if you keep reading and growing. Ideas come to those who have read, thought and prayed. They come to the mind that has been prepared, furrowed, fertilized and watered. Never say that you have no time for reading and meditating because you always find time for the things you really want to do. If your interest is fishing or golf or skiing, you will not leave a stone unturned until you find time for it. The best way to find time for sermon preparation is to rise early and get to your desk with your boots on (not slippers), ready to do serious work. All the great preachers were extremely busy men, but they set aside the best hours of the day for study. Be prepared to spend at least ten to fifteen hours on sermon preparation each week: two to three hours each morning, Monday through Friday. It will sharpen your understanding and fill your mind. In writing to Timothy, Paul says, "When you come...bring the books and above all the parchments" (2 Tim 4.13). Books were important to Paul.

Francis Bacon said once, "Good reading maketh a full man." If you read fifteen hours a week, you will not have to spend fifteen hours each week on your sermon. Thoughts, ideas, illustrations will come to you for your sermon from the fullness of your general reading.

There is a difference between tactics and strategy. It has been said that in World War I the Germans were superior in tactics, but the Allies were superior in strategy. Tactics is what it takes to win a single battle. Strategy is the master plan that wins the war. A preacher who reads only to prepare next Sunday's sermon is dealing with tactics. The preacher, however, who reads not just to prepare for the next sermon, but to enrich himself and grow spiritually will be preparing not for one Sunday, but for all the Sundays that lie ahead. His reading will benefit and inspire all his sermons. Such a preacher has good strategy.

Jim Bishop once said of his books, "I'm rich in friends. In this house I'm surrounded by 4,000 of them. They sit quietly on shelves from floor to ceiling. The upkeep is nothing. When I take a book down and open it, it speaks eloquently for as long as I please. It forms, it edifies.... Time does not mute beauty of speech."

Let me share with you the following story because it emphasizes greatly the importance of reading. A man got up early one morning to cut down trees. He worked eight hours and cut down thirty trees. He was satisfied but felt he could bring down more if he would skip lunch. He did, but he brought down only twenty-five trees— five less than the day before even though he had worked longer and harder. He decided the next day he would start two hours earlier in addition to skipping lunch in order to achieve his goal. He did, but even though he had worked two hours longer, he cut down only twenty trees—ten less than the first day. Can you guess what he was doing wrong? Simple! He forgot to sharpen the ax! We may work harder and longer in our sermon preparation, but unless we sharpen the ax daily through reading, prayer and meditation, we shall be accomplishing less and less.

What the Church Fathers Did

What was the attitude of the Church Fathers toward study and reading? The rule of Saint Anthony witnesses to a close connection between prayer and reading. The first rule is: "Before all, pray without interruption...." And the second rule is: "...pray and read perpetually." Have you ever noticed that when you're bent over your desk in study, you're also in a posture of prayer? The rabbis used to say that an hour of studying God's word is, in the sight of God, as an hour of prayer.

The Church Fathers loved reading, especially the Scriptures, which they memorized by heart. Saint Isaak of Nineveh wrote, "A true spirituality is drawn from the bottomless treasure of the Scriptures." Even during mealtime there were readings for the monks, providing them with food for the soul. In some monasteries, where poverty was applied in the strictest sense, an allowance was made for books. This sets a good precedent for us today. Every parish should have an established book allowance for its priest. In some monasteries books were also placed in front of the iconostasis for the brothers to take and read. Strict rules were established to protect books and libraries.

What To Read

While in seminary, the New Testament and Old Testament courses introduced us to the Scriptures. After seminary we should go out and, for the rest of our lives, keep diving into the Scriptures through personal study and meditation until they become part of us. As Paul writes to Timothy, "Do your best to present yourself to God as one approved, a workman who has no need to be ashamed, rightly handling the word of truth" (2 Tim 2.15).

In seminary, Patrology (the study of the Fathers) introduced us to the Church Fathers and their writings. After seminary we should go out and read them, drench our minds and hearts in them.

I have never met Saint John Chrysostom, but I can sit down and have a heart-to-heart, mind-to-mind chat with him through his writings. I have never met Saint Basil personally, but I can sit down in his company and let him speak to me through his great writings. To study the lives and commune with the thoughts of the great saints of this world is a sacred discipline that will yield the richest fruits in the ministry of God's servants. We forfeit great wisdom if we do not seek to converse with the inspiring thoughts of God's great saints of the past. So, buy a set of the Church Fathers and read a page or two each day. The next best thing to being great is walking with the great.

An important practice in Orthodox monasticism is the concept of the spiritual father. Every monk must have a spiritual father to guide him in his spiritual life. Every priest can have more than one such spiritual father guiding him in his ministry of preaching and teaching if he communes regularly with the great Fathers of the Church through their writings. Imagine going through an entire year when Saint Symeon the New Theologian is your spiritual father, another year when Saint Gregory of Nyssa is your spiritual father, etc.. How richly your ministry would be blessed!

In addition to Scripture and the Church Fathers, another great source of preaching insights are the services of the Orthodox Church. Read the Pentekostarion, the Triodion, the 'Festal Menaion.' Read them daily as part of your devotions. Pray them! The entire theology of the Orthodox Church is found in its superb hymnology.

I share with you what Father George Florovsky has written about the study of the Church Fathers:

> I have often a strange feeling. When I read the ancient classics of Christian theology, the Fathers of the Church, I find them more relevant to the troubles and problems of my own time than the production of modern theologians. The Fathers were wrestling with existential problems, with those revelations of the eternal issues which were described and recorded in Holy Scripture. I would risk a suggestion that Saint Athanasios and Saint Augustine are much

more up to date than many of our theological con-
temporaries. The reason is very simple: they were
dealing with things and not with maps; they were
concerned not so much with what man can believe
as with what God has done for man.[39]

In addition to the Scriptures, the Church Fathers and
the hymnology of our Church, it is important that the
preacher read the great sermons of past masters—not just
to read them, but to analyze them sentence by sentence,
thought by thought, to see what made them great. I met a
priest once who told me that he never read the sermons of
others. He considered it dishonest. That attitude is com-
parable to an architect never looking at any other house or
building that has been erected, or a student surgeon never
observing a master surgeon at work. We can learn much
by studying the works of others in our field.[40] Each great
preacher has something to teach us if we are willing to
learn. Another excellent suggestion is to read at least one
good book on preaching every year. I have been doing this
for years and have found it to be of immense help in my
preaching ministry.

A good rule for the preacher to follow is always to give
credit when making substantial use of another person's
material. I leave you with two questions on the subject
of originality: How can you grow intellectually and spiritually unless you struggle with yourself and the material
the Church has handed on to you for interpretation and

---

[39]   *Bible, Church, Tradition.*

[40]   We recommend the encyclopedia *Twenty Centuries of Great
Christian Preaching,* eds. Fant and Pinson (Waco, Texas, 1971).

application to your day and age? How can you discover what original and significant contribution God can make through you if you do not produce your own material?

Hold on to What You Read

It is not enough to read widely. One must learn how to preserve what is read so that it is readily available when needed. Forgetting what one reads is a perennial problem. A Muslim scholar complained that even though he studied the Koran, it kept slipping away from him "like a camel whose leg was not tied." It is not what we read, but what we remember that makes us learned.

St. Isaak the Syrian wrote, "When you receive a good thought in your mind, force it down into your heart and keep it there."

> Why can't I retain
> The things that I learn
> And be more elite?
> Instead—it's quite plain
> How well I retain
> The things that I eat!
>   *Jean B. Boyce*

How much wiser we would be if we retained as much of what we learn as what we eat. We lose hundreds of good ideas by not capturing them at the moment we have them and making sure we can refer to them when they are needed.

How can we retain what we read?

1. Always carry a small note pad or set of index cards with you when you are reading. If you come across a noteworthy idea, illustration or anecdote, jot down the subject

on the pad, i.e., 'anger.' Then write the title of the book, the author and the page number. I have always kept small index cards in my billfold. When I hear a good thought or sermon idea on the radio or in a conversation, I immediately jot it down on the card for filing. When one great preacher of old was on walks or riding horseback, he would jot down ideas for sermons and pin them to his coat. When he returned home, he would write out fuller explanations of the notes on the same scraps of paper. Sometimes his whole coat was covered with pieces of paper.

One should never read, or sleep or be anywhere without paper and pen. The Holy Spirit works even through our unconscious mind and often inspires us with thoughts and ideas when we awake in the middle of the night. These should be recorded immediately. Such a practice will prove invaluable in the preparation of sermons. Start on it immediately and stick to it.

In addition to a small note pad, a good pair of scissors will prove to be a good friend in sermon preparation. Clip out articles or ideas from newspapers and magazines and paste them in a scrap book. This is especially useful if the clipping is good for more than one topic, i.e., 'anger,' 'love your enemy,' 'forgiveness,' etc. Paste the clipping in your scrap book. Then write on a piece of paper the topic, the page number of the scrap book and the number of the scrap book itself if you have more than one such book. The paper would thus read, "'anger,' see p. 10, scrap book number 3." Then place the paper aside for filing.

2. Set up a good filing system for all the above slips of paper, magazine articles, etc.. It should be a simple system that will not require you to leave the ministry in order to

find time enough to keep it going. I have found it effective to establish one filing system of manilla folders for the Sunday Gospel and Epistle lessons. Any ideas relating to the lessons are accumulated in a box and placed in the proper folder at least once each month or two. A second file is kept for topics I should like to preach on. This topical file is alphabetical. For example, if I decide to preach on 'happiness,' I will refer to the folder under 'H' marked 'happiness' where I may have been placing clippings and ideas for the past twenty years. I will usually find in this folder far more material than I need for a single sermon. Sometimes there is even enough accumulated material to write a book on the subject. One great preacher said that it took twenty years for one of his sermons to mature in his folder. As a gardener keeps many plants growing in various beds, so the preacher can cultivate a multitude of seeds or ideas and keep developing them in his files.

Writing the Sermon

Beverley Nichols, who had just written his very successful book *Prelude*, told of meeting Winston Churchill. "How long did it take to write?" asked Churchill. Nichols replied that he did not know, that it was done in patches over a period of five or six months. "Didn't you work on it regularly?" Winston demanded. Nichols replied that he could not write regularly, that he had to wait for the right mood. "Nonsense," said Churchill, "You should go to your room every day at 9 o'clock and say, 'I am going to write for three hours.' "

When Nichols asked what happened when one found one could not write, if one had a headache or indigestion,

Churchill answered, "You've got to get over that. If you sit waiting for inspiration, you will sit waiting till you are an old man. Writing is like any other job, like marching an army, for instance. If you sit down and wait till the weather is fine, you won't get far with your troops. Kick yourself, irritate yourself, but write; it's the only way."

Most good speakers and preachers first write out their entire speech and then rehearse the material until it is so set in their minds that they can 'talk' it or use only brief notes or even no notes at all. One of the greatest American preachers, Fosdick, said that in forty years of preaching he had never given a sermon that he had not first written out fully. Whether you take the manuscript to the pulpit or not, writing it out will insure that you will have something of value to say.

There are many advantages to writing the sermon. First, the time allocated to preaching in the liturgy is short, perhaps ten, certainly not more than fifteen, minutes—the shorter, the better. If the sermon is written, you have complete control over its length and you can make each word count to the maximum. Secondly, once written, the sermon is never lost. It can be used again and even published if need be. Thirdly, writing increases precision of thought and speech. It enhances beauty and clarity of style. Fourthly, even the so-called 'extemporaneous' sermon is best when it has been written out beforehand. It will be well organized, logical and forceful.

A good plan to use in writing the sermon, though not the only one, is the following:

1. Begin your sermon preparation early. Monday is not too soon. Select your text, meditate on it, consult the commentaries and the Church Fathers. Make written notes as you read and ponder, especially of noteworthy and relevant illustrations.

2. Make a clear, logical outline of the sermon.

3. Think through the outline, revising it as needed.

4. Write out the sermon in full, being especially careful to use the living language of speech, not of books.

5. If you plan to deliver the sermon from notes or memory, you may reduce the outline to key words and phrases to help you remember it.

A clergyman's small daughter watched him preparing his sermon. "Daddy," she asked, "does God tell you what to say?" "Yes, he does, dear," he replied. "Why?"

"I was wondering why you cross out so much of it," she said.

4
Crafting the Sermon

It has been said that the two requirements of a good sermon are: 1) a good beginning and a good ending, and 2) keeping the two as close as possible.

Someone said that the recipe for a good sermon should always include an ample amount of shortening.

The optimist has been defined as one who thinks the preacher is nearly through when he says, "Finally."

When asked about the church service, a little girl replied, "The music was nice, but the commercial was too long."

A little boy in church, awaking after a nap, asked his father, "Has the preacher finished yet?" "Yes, son, he has finished, but he hasn't stopped."

Someone asked, "How was the sermon today?" "Fine," was the reply, "but the preacher missed several good stopping places."

One Sunday morning a minister apologized to his congregation for the bandage on his face. "I was thinking about my sermon while shaving," he explained, "and cut my face."

Afterward, in the collection plate, he found a note: "Next time, why not think about your face and cut the sermon." Einstein said once, after listening to a long-winded preacher, "I have just discovered a new theory of relativity."

One wag said, "Lawyers are not the only people who can write a 10,000-word document and call it a brief."

In sixteenth-century England they were pretty blunt about the length of a sermon. Many churches installed hour glasses which were attached to the pulpits and could be seen by both preachers and worshipers!

The many jokes relative to the length of sermons should speak to us loud and clear about a subject that has caused problems to worshipers for many centuries.

In looking through Scripture for guidance on this subject, all I could find was a verse in the book of Ecclesiastes which says, "Let thy speech be short, comprehending much in few words."

It is always important to stop speaking before the audience stops listening. Adlai Stevenson brought this out when he spoke to the students of Princeton University in 1963. He said, "I understand I am here to speak and you are here to listen. Let's hope we both finish at the same time." A good speaker is one who knows all the advantages of stopping sooner than his audience expects him to.

Brevity is even more necessary today due to the fact that we are 'over communicated.' We are drowning in a sea of words. Someone said that driving through Los Angeles with all its billboards was like driving through a dictionary. Our attention span has been shortened due to several factors. People today are oriented to short features, spot

announcements, vignettes and programs constantly interrupted by commercials and other breaks. Radio, television
and roadside signs clamor for our attention by allowing us
to get the essence of a message in a very short period of
time.

Experiments at Michigan State University show that it
is possible to condense a fifty-five minute lecture to seven
and a half minutes with no significant difference in recall
of basic facts. Personally, I have had to condense many
fifteen-minute sermons to thirty-five seconds for an inspirational spot on our local CBS television station. It is
a discipline that has helped me immensely. Television is
slowly teaching us that good preaching can be done in a
shorter period of time.

Looking back over his ministry, one retired preacher said, "If I were living my ministry over again, I would
discipline myself to preach shorter sermons. I would not
preach less Gospel, I would just preach as much Gospel in
a shorter time. As I look back over many of the sermons
I have preached, I see that there was injected into many
of them material that was not really necessary. It was put
there for entertainment, or as a filler or for some reason
other than a direct effort to communicate the Gospel to
the hearers."

I can just hear someone who has read some of my long
sermons say to me, "Physician, heal thyself." I must explain
that these long sermons were not delivered all at once, but
over a three– or four–week period in time segments of
from twelve to fourteen minutes each.

Louis Cassels, an experienced writer for UPS, has said,
"In UPS we have found from expensive and costly reader-

ship surveys that there is an inverse correlation between the length of a news feature and the number of readers it attracts. We also have learned why most articles will be written too long unless their writers are compelled to tighten them up. The reason is simply that it's much easier to be verbose than to be succinct." There is a rule in architecture which says, "Less is more." There is more in less. There is beauty in simplicity, as well as in brevity. Look at the Parthenon as an example—beauty in simplicity! Certainly the same can hold true in preaching. I forget who it was who said, "Half of art is knowing when to stop."

Short is beautiful! I invite you to look up some truly great one-sentence sermons in Scripture, i.e., John 3.16, Revelation 1.5-6 and Philippians 4.6. There are many more!

Three of the world's greatest literary treasures are less than 300 words: The Lord's Prayer, the Twenty-Third Psalm and Lincoln's Gettysburg Address. Short is beautiful!

When Woodrow Wilson was asked by a friend to speak at a certain convention, he asked to know how much time he was expected to fill.

"Why, Mr. Wilson," the friend replied, "with your vast knowledge as a professor and political scientist, what difference does it make whether you are scheduled for sixty minutes or thirty minutes?"

Mr. Wilson shook his head and is reputed to have said, "If I am to talk an hour, then I could compose the speech in a couple of days. But a thirty-minute address would require a week. And to speak ten minutes I'd need a month's preparation." The same is true in preaching. The shorter it is to be, the more work is required to make sure that every word produces maximum effect.

We must point out also that the reason many people find preaching to be unbearable is not simply because it is too long. An even greater reason is that too much preaching is unbelievably trite and addresses no issue of significance.

I conclude this section on the desirable length of a sermon by sharing with you these words by the authors of *Word and Table*: "Preaching may gain in strength by being shortened and sharply focused."

The All-Important Question: How?

Thomas Carlyle, bored by long, dull sermons, said to his mother one day, "If I had to preach I would go into the pulpit and say no more than this: 'All you good people know what you ought to do; well, go home and do it.' " His mother, knitting by the fireside, thought for a while in silence and then said, "Aye, Thomas, and would you tell them how?"

A centipede, suffering from arthritis, went to the wise old owl for advice. The owl thought for a long time and then replied: "Centipede, you have one hundred legs swollen with arthritis. My advice is that you change yourself into a stork. With only two legs you would cut your pain by ninety-eight percent. Then by using your wings to stay off your legs, you wouldn't have any trouble at all." The centipede was delighted with the suggestion and asked the wise old owl how he could change into a stork. The owl quickly replied, "Oh, I wouldn't know about the details. I offer only general policy."

The trouble with much preaching is that it is long on 'general policy' and short on 'how' to achieve and implement that policy. It is not enough to say that something should be done; we must proceed to show specifically and in detail how it can be done.

Halford Luccock, the famous Yale professor of homiletics, tells of installing a hot water heater in his summer cottage at the lake. "When I got there in August it was all installed.... It was a beauty, but it wasn't running. I wanted to use it, and then to my joy I saw attached to it what I thought was a set of directions. That is where I made my mistake. It wasn't a set of directions, but a set of tributes beautifully printed in red and blue, telling me that the heater was (1) safe, (2) quick, (3) efficient, (4) tamper-proof, (5) economical and (6) dependable. I said yes, but how does the thing work? What do I do to use it to get some hot water? Not a word on what to do. I would have traded all six eloquent tributes for three clear words of direction."[41]

Consider how frustrated the pilgrim became in *The Way of the Pilgrim* as he searched to discover how he could pray ceaselessly. Listen to his testimony:

> I thought to myself, What shall I do? Where can I find someone who will teach me? I decided to visit all the churches that were renowned for their preaching in the hope of hearing something that would make things clear for me. This is what I did, and I heard many excellent sermons on prayer telling what prayer is and how necessary it is and what

---

41   H. E. Luccock, *Living without Gloves* (New York, 1957).

are the fruits of prayer. But no one told me how I could pray unceasingly. I did hear one sermon on continual and uninterrupted prayer, but nothing was said about the means to reach that state. And so I stopped going to public sermons because I could not find in them what I was looking for. I decided instead to search with God's help for a man of great learning and experience who could teach me privately how to obtain what my heart longed for so desperately.[42]

We must remember constantly what has been called the preacher's most forgotten word—'how!' How can a person achieve what I have talked about in my sermon today? How? It is the question Mary asked of the angel at the Annunciation: "How can this be, since I have no husband?" (Lk 1.34).

We must not merely tell our people to love God more; we must also show them how they can love him more. We must not merely tell them that they ought to pray; we must show them how to pray. We must not merely urge them to live closer to God; we must show them how they can draw closer to God. We must not merely call on them to love their enemy; we must show them how and with whose power they can love their enemy. We must not tell them merely to behave more lovingly toward their family; we must show them how. How incomplete, how frustrating, how depressing is a sermon that does not lead us to the source of power in order to answer the all- important question—how? "How can this be...?" Mary asked the angel. The answer came swiftly: "The Holy Spirit will come

---

42   *The Way of the Pilgrim*, trans. R.M. French (London, 1960).

upon you, and the power of the Most High will overshad-
ow you..." There is the answer to the 'how?'—then as now,
'the Holy Spirit.' "...you shall receive power when the Holy
Spirit has come upon you" (Acts 1.8).

One Central Point

In his book *Pictorial Composition* Henry R. Poore writes,
"The most absolute and the most important idea in the
production of art is...that one idea shall be supreme." In
any single work of art there cannot be two or more ideas
of equal importance. There has to be one main idea, and
anything that confuses that idea, or distracts attention
from it, has to be eliminated.

In the old days some of us were taught that each sermon should be broken down into three points or parts.
Today we have learned that people have a hard enough
time remembering one point, let alone three. It is far more
effective to have one central point in the sermon and to
emphasize that one point often through repetition, much
like the recurring theme of a Beethoven symphony. It ties
the whole symphony together in a single unit.

Before you can make a point in a sermon, you must be
sure you know exactly what that point is. You must begin
by writing it out in a single sentence that is short, concise,
clear and understandable. If you cannot express the main
point of your sermon in one short sentence, you should
not proceed with the sermon until such time as you can.
The trouble with many sermons is that the preacher has
no point and is not trying to make a point. He is just ram-
bling on aimlessly.

This is why no sermon should be written before the
question is asked, "What is my purpose in this sermon?
What am I trying to accomplish?" Not one step should be
taken until you have answered that question with a simple
one-sentence statement which will, in effect, be the point
of the whole sermon. If you can't do it in one sentence,
chances are you are going to be preaching in vague generalities. If you can't express the essence of your sermon
in one short sentence, what will the listener remember
if he is asked during the week, "Now, what was the sermon all about?" If you can express it in one sentence, in
most cases you will be able to transmit that one sentence,
that one main point, to your listeners in such a way that
they will remember it even years later. One person tells
of remembering a sermon preached thirty years ago because the preacher had one main thought which he kept
repeating in many different words, phrases and sentences.
"I remember it," he says, "because of the many interesting
ways in which he repeated the one idea that he wanted us
to carry away with us."

Advertising writers will work for a whole week trying
to come up with a single six-word slogan. They know how
important that one-sentence slogan is in influencing people, especially when it is repeated often.

We need to appreciate the value of repetition in a
sermon. An outstanding trial lawyer said to his pastor:
"Preachers often fail to make themselves understood by
not repeating enough. When I address a jury, I always repeat the points of my argument at least twice in order to
impress them upon the minds of the jury. I have, upon
occasion, repeated things as many times as there were ju-

rymen before me. If I failed to repeat, I would fail to win the verdict I wanted."

Saint John of Damascus used repetition with great effect in his hymnology. Specifically, the *kanons* have been described as "hymns of praise in an exultant or scatological mood, expressing dogmatic ideas by means of reiteration and variation. These highly elaborate repetitions produce in the listener a mystical mood, which was intensified by the solemnity of the ritual and the visual impression of the icons."[43] Repetition is used most effectively in our church hymns. An example of this is the following Paschal troparion:

> A sacred Pascha has been shown forth to us:
> A new and holy Pascha,
> A mystic Pascha,
> An all-venerable Pascha,
> A Pascha which is Christ the Redeemer;
> A spotless Pascha,
> A great Pascha,
> A Pascha of the faithful,
> A Pascha which has opened to us the gates of Paradise,
> A Pascha which hallows all the faithful.

One great preacher said, "If anyone desires to lodge an idea in the minds of his hearers, he must learn the secret of artistic repetition, by which the same thing is said over and over again, but cast into a new dress on each appearance."[44]

---

[43]   E. Wellesz, *Byzantine Music and Hymnography* (Oxford, 1961).

[44]   John Watson, *The Cure of Souls* (New York, 1896).

The value of repetition is brought out by the old practice in planting of putting three beans in one hole: one for the worm, one for the crow and one to live and produce a crop. Remembering Jesus' parable of the soils, we must make allowance for the seeds that will be lost due to the poor condition of the soil into which they will fall. We must keep repeating line by line, precept by precept, the truth that we would teach until it becomes impossible to forget.

In summary, every sermon must have a target, and that target is expressed in the one main point of the sermon. In order to be on target the preacher must aim at a single squirrel rather than at the whole tree. Instead of splattering the congregation with homiletical buckshot in a shotgun approach, he must aim at the heart. If the theme is too big, such as prayer, cut it down to bite-size pieces so that people can be nourished. In the case of prayer, the subject can be broken down into how to pray, why pray, what to pray for, etc. By trying to exhaust a subject in one sermon, preachers merely exhaust themselves and their congregation.

One preacher said, "I find the getting of that one main sentence expressing the essence of the sermon the hardest, most exciting and the most fruitful labor of my study."

So, give some loving care to the organization of your sermon. Tell your people in a single sentence what you are going to say. Say it. Tell them what you have said. Repeat. Connect. Emphasize. Keep it constantly tied together. Wind it up by saying in the conclusion, "The point I am trying to make is this...." They will get the point.

The Use of Illustrations

A rabbi, famous for his learning and his wit, was once asked by his students why he so often illustrated a truth by telling a story:

> That I can do best by telling a story [he said], a parable about Parable itself. There was a time when Truth went among men unadorned, as naked as his name. And whoever saw Truth turned away, in fear or in shame, and gave him no welcome.
>
> So Truth wandered through the lands of the earth, rebuffed and unwanted.
>
> One day, most disconsolate, he met Parable strolling along happily in fine and many-colored garb. 'Truth, why do you seem so sad?' asked Parable cheerfully.
>
> 'Because I am so old and ugly that all men avoid me,' replied Truth.
>
> 'Nonsense,' laughed Parable. 'That is not why men avoid you. Here, borrow some of my clothes and see what happens.'
>
> So Truth donned some of Parable's lovely garments and, lo, everywhere he went, he was welcomed.
>
> [The rabbi smiled and said] For the truth is that men cannot face Truth naked; they much prefer him disguised.

When Immanuel Kant sent a draft of his 750-page *Critique of Pure Reason* to a friend for critical appraisal, the colleague wrote back, "I'll go mad if I try to finish reading this. You have included no illustrations." But Kant felt he would never be able to finish the manuscript if he stopped to illustrate his points. The result was that he produced a work that was cumbersome even for a philosopher friend.

It has been said that one picture is worth 10,000 words. But recent research at Ohio University explored the question of whether sharp photographs would be rated by readers as having more emotional impact than detailed verbal descriptions of the pictured event. The study discovered that, contrary to prediction, verbal descriptions, word pictures, on the whole actually received slightly higher ratings than actual pictures. The report did assert, however, that photographs do help to grab the person's attention more quickly.

The preacher's function is to turn the ear into an eye so that what is heard may also be seen. The preacher is called to be an artist painting pictures with words. In the words of Halford Luccock we need "to give our message a sight track, as well as a sound track. In our presentation, to give something for the eye, as well as for the ear."[45]

Jesus joined sight and sound, the ear and the eye, through his extensive use of parables. He turned on the lights, illuminating his sermons with numerous illustrations. He painted beautiful pictures with words so that people could not only hear, but also see the truth. "All this Jesus said to the crowds in parables; indeed, he said nothing to them without a parable" (Mt 13.34).

God becomes real to people not through abstractions, but through persons and through the concrete situations of everyday life. Jesus communicated what the kingdom of God was like most eloquently through parables taken

---

[45]   Halford Luccock, Communicating the Gospel (New York, 1954).

from everyday life. He used word pictures. He referred to
God not in abstractions like the Ground of all Being, In-
finite, Changeless, Impassible, the Transcendent One, the
Omniscient Originator and Ruler of the Universe. Instead,
he said that God was like a Sower, a Mustard Seed, a Pearl
of great price, a Father who received his son who had deliberately left his house, a Woman who had lost a coin, a
Shepherd who sought a lost sheep, a Fisherman casting his
net into the sea, Yeast, Good Seed, Hidden Treasure, etc..
He told us that God was Spirit, the Bread of Life, the Light
of the World, the Door of the Sheep, etc..

Jesus painted word pictures with his parables. And it
is hard to forget those word pictures because people will
remember a picture long after they have forgotten an argument. If you have occasion to preach a sermon twice to
the same congregation, even if it is after a period of years,
try not to use the same illustrations. People will invariably
remember them. They will not remember the logical argu-
ments you used or the fancy language, but only the word
pictures you painted, the illustrations. This is an example
of just how effective an illustration is. And, by the way, the
use of illustrations in a sermon is very Orthodox. For what
are illustrations but verbal icons.

An illustration, a parable, a story can take a more-or-
less abstract idea and give it shape, color, flavor, aroma,
music and warmth. It can give the idea a soul and make it
come alive.

We need to exert some caution in the use of illustrations. First, never draw an illustration from your counseling with parishioners. One pastor found that he held
the attention of his audience very well when he began: "I

was talking to a young man this week about his sex life..."
After that, hardly anyone came to him for counseling. No
one wants to wonder if his confidential statement to the
priest will become next Sunday's sermon illustration. Secondly, an illustration that needs explanation is worthless.
A lamp should do its own work. It should not attract attention to itself. An illustration that attracts too much attention to itself will distract the listeners attention from
the main point of the sermon. Such illustrations should be
avoided. Good illustrations are like street lamps—scarce-
ly noticed but throwing floods of light upon the road.
Thirdly, illustrations are like windows. They let in light.
Every house needs windows, but be careful not to make
the whole house just one window after another. We need
walls, too. A sermon should not degenerate into a string
of illustrations or anecdotes. Finally, no quotation, illustration or anecdote should ever be used just for its own
sake, but only because it enhances the purpose of the sermon: to explain a truth that would otherwise be difficult
to understand.

Most good preachers derive illustrations not so much
from sermon illustration books as from their extensive
reading and their constant observation, with a penetrating
eye, of the ordinary things that happen about them.

One famous American preacher, Henry Ward Beecher,
said that his preaching improved greatly when he began to
pay more attention to illustrations: "I can say...that while
illustrations are as natural to me as breathing, I use fifty
now, as compared to one in the early years of my ministry." As preachers we cannot but follow the example of our

Master who spoke in parables, "Indeed, he said nothing to them without a parable" (Mt 13.34).

A Holy Imagination

One of the ingredients necessary for crafting a good sermon is a holy imagination—an imagination, which under the guidance and inspiration of the Holy Spirit, seeks to enter the mind and heart of those about whom we speak. The Fathers of the Church speak of such a divinely inspired imagination.

For example, Abba Isaak said, "Once I was sitting with Abba Poimen, and I saw that he was in ecstasy; and since I used to speak very openly with him, I prostrated before him and asked him, 'Tell me, where were you?' And he did not want to tell me. But when I pressed him, he replied, 'My thoughts were with Saint Mary, the Mother of God, as she stood and wept at the cross of the Savior; and I wish that I could always weep as much as she wept then.' " Abba Poimen was actually standing with Mary under the cross, experiencing her sorrow at the sight of her Son on the cross!

Saint Ambrose also speaks of a holy imagination when he addresses the catechumens in the Early Church:

> Now I want each one of you to think of himself as that blind man. Consider the eyes of your spirit, how blind they were at one time to the things of God and to the new life offered in the sacraments, how you could see only the outward signs and not the inward reality. Then one day you met Jesus. He took clay and applied it to your eyes. 'When was that?', you ask. It was the day you gave in your name as a can-

didate for baptism and joined the class of learners.
That was the beginning of the whole process of your
enlightenment. You learned to recognize all that was
wrong in your life, to repent of your sins and confess
them, acknowledging the condition in which all of us
are born blind to the light of God's grace.[46]

We must pray for such a sacred imagination as we read
and study for the preparation of our sermons. We are
called not just to speak abstractly about the plight of the
blind man, but to enter his mind and heart by identifying
ourselves with him as Saint Ambrose states so well.

Feedback

Receiving some kind of feedback from the pew is all-
important for the successful communication of the Gospel.

Of course, we are receiving such feedback constantly
as we look out to the congregation. Chesterton observed
once that a yawn is a silent shout. It cannot and should not
be ignored. While it may be bad manners, you'll have to
admit, a yawn certainly is an honest opinion.

One preacher was asked if the behavior of his congregation during the service bothered him. He replied, "Well, I
was considerably disturbed on a recent Sunday when early in the sermon an elderly lady down front removed her
hearing aid from her ear and quietly put it in her purse."

Another clergyman reached the point of frustration and
chided his listeners: "I do not mind you looking at your
watches from time to time, but when you hold them up to

---

[46]   Saint Ambrose, *Sermon 14*.

your ears and shake them to determine whether they're still running, that's going a trifle too far!"

We must learn to appreciate the many forms that feedback takes. We need to learn from it. It is saying something important to us. If we heed it, we can greatly improve our preaching. One preacher says that while preaching, he never takes his eyes off the congregation, looking for many subtle, and not so subtle, signs of feedback: a yawn, a far-away look in the eyes, half- closed eyes, etc.. I remember one priest, coming back to preach at a parish he had served for many years, who said to them, "I have a nodding acquaintance with many of you."

To benefit from feedback we must be secure enough in Christ and humble enough to really listen to it and seek it out. We must realize that it will not always be positive feedback. If your preaching is criticized, remember that when Jesus preached his first sermon, he finished no more than the first few sentences before the audience, "filled with wrath, rose up and thrust him out of the city" (Lk 4.28-29) and attempted to murder him. The success of a sermon does not always depend on the Trendex rating, but on whether it brings people under conviction so they will turn to Christ or turn from him. And sometimes they will turn from Christ and against us. This is one kind of feedback we must always expect and not be surprised by when it comes.

But there are other forms of feedback that we must constantly seek out so that our preaching is not a monologue, but a dialogue with our listeners. Let us examine some of these forms:

1. There is the feedback that comes directly and sometimes rather spontaneously from the congregation. There
is some evidence of spontaneous participation by the
people in the preaching of the Church Fathers, especially
Augustine and Chrysostom. Augustine was known to ask
questions of the people present if he wanted to impress
upon them the importance of what he was saying. In his
De Doctrina Christiana he explicitly advocates this practice.[47] Augustine also made his listeners repeat scriptural
passages after him. While preaching a sermon, he would
say, "Now all say after me..." Often people would voice
their approval or disapproval of what he said by shouting
acclamations or beating their breasts, for example, when
Augustine spoke of the need for contrition. Perhaps some
of us would not tolerate such forms of acclamation or response in our Liturgy today; but for the popular and uneducated audiences to whom Augustine preached, such
responses were a form of dialogue with the preacher and
offered some good feedback.

Much of this also holds true for Saint Chrysostom.
His audience often applauded him, shouted out acclamations or repeated passages from Scripture by heart after
Chrysostom had read familiar verses to them. And, of
course, they applauded him, as was the custom of the time.

From what we have seen, then, there is some historical
basis from the apostolic and patristic eras for participation by the people in the sermon. Rather than merely imi-
tate the apostolic and patristic modes of responding to the
sermon, our living liturgical tradition today may wish to

---

[47]   4.39

develop its own forms of lay response in order to provide much-needed feedback.

One great German preacher spoke of his need of a response from the congregation when he said:

> I had to preach with body, mind and soul, as the apostle Paul says, in intimate contact with the congregation. I had to demand something of the congregation. I had to be able to see in their faces whether what I said in the name of my Lord Jesus Christ was reaching them or not. And from the way the congregation said the 'amen' I had to be able to sense whether the sermon had gone home. With the 'amen' I was released from the inner tension in which I had lived during the preceding twenty-four hours.

2. In addition to the feedback that comes directly from the congregation, there is that which we must seek out ourselves. This will take many forms. First, there is the 'Gospel talk-back group.' This is a group of interested persons who are invited to sit at a certain table or meet in a certain room during the coffee hour following the Liturgy. Here they are allowed to ask questions and share together on the subject that was addressed in the sermon. The same may be accomplished during the prayer and Bible study groups that meet during the week. During these meetings the priest may seek out feedback to his homily by asking if there are any questions or comments on the subject of last Sunday's sermon.

The task of the Church is to proclaim the good news, but we must pay careful attention to what happens to the lay people who do the listening and the receiving most of the time. Are they listening? Do they have any response to make? Are they being allowed to make that response?

One way of seeking out their response is by asking them questions. This is the form Father Dudko uses in his book of sermons entitled *Our Hope*.[48] He asked his parishioners to submit questions to him on religious topics. His sermons consist of the answers he gives to their questions. Such a method assures the preacher that he is speaking to the real needs of his people. Such feedback for future sermon topics may be elicited through the use of questionnaires such as the one that follows:

SERMON QUESTIONNAIRE

This is to request your suggestions for sermons. What areas of interest or need would you like to have treated in future sermons? If you will indicate your suggestions, the pastor will try to address himself to these subjects in the months to come.

Doctrine: *What do we believe?*—Are there any particular beliefs about which you are uncertain or troubled (e.g., God, Christ, ourselves, destiny)?

_____   _____

_____   _____

_____   _____

Personal Adjustment: *How can I live more effectively?*— In what personal problems do you think religion can offer help (e.g., anxiety, fear, sorrow)?

_____   _____

_____   _____

_____   _____

---

[48]   Fr. Dudko, *Our Hope* (New York, 1977).

Morality: *How should Christians behave?*—What moral problems do you think are especially tense today and open to Christian guidance (e.g., honesty, chastity, temperance)?

_____   _____

_____   _____

_____   _____

Social Issues: *How can we be Christian in relation to others?*—Where are the main social problems which concern you (e.g., family, racial issues, politics)?

_____   _____

_____   _____

_____   _____

Bible: *What does the Bible say?*—What sections of the Bible are of interest to you (e.g., prophets, life of Jesus, teachings of Jesus, Paul)?

_____   _____

_____   _____

_____   _____

Another way of testing the effectiveness of our preaching is by inviting people to come to confession immediately following a sermon on repentance. Or the pastor may say to the congregation following the Sunday sermon: "I believe there are some in the congregation this morning who are in great trouble. I invite any man, woman, or young person who is in great need to meet me at the end of the Liturgy in the following room—We shall pray together and offer the sacraments of unction and penance to those who need them." One pastor reported that he found about forty people in the room one Sunday. He offered a general prayer for all of them, assuring them of God's personal love. He discovered in the group people with all kinds of needs to which he was able to minister during the week.

Another form of feedback that is solicited by some pastors comes from the so-called 'sermon feed-in group.' This is a select group of about four to six persons recruited by the pastor to provide feed-in material for a selected topic or scriptural passage before the sermon is preached and thus aid in the construction of the sermon. Members of the group may rotate with a new member coming in each week and staying on for four weeks. The group meets early in the week for a two-hour session with the pastor. The first ten or so minutes are devoted to comments on last Sunday's sermon. Then the pastor provides the necessary exegetical material on the passage to be preached on the following Sunday. He then listens to the group's input. Such a group assures that the needs of the congregation will be better met because the pastor will be meeting with members of the congregation who will be sharing those needs with him.

Another source of good feedback for the homily is the pastor's wife. In my preaching ministry some of the severest and most constructive criticism has always come from my wife who has also been a truly important spiritual partner in my ministry. When the late Archbishop Michael ordained me into the priesthood, he assured my wife that she, too, had been 'ordained.' I can testify from experience that she, too, was indeed 'ordained' when I was. Some of the finest criticism and feed- back—both positive and negative, but always constructive and loving—has come from her.

Finally, in evaluating the sermon after it is preached, the pastor or the 'sermon-feed-in-group' may use the following guidelines which are adapted from O.S. Davis' *Principles of Preaching*:[49]

> *In studying a sermon, these factors should be considered:*
>
> Overall Impression: Was the sermon interesting? Informative? Moving? Convincing?
>
> Analysis: Outline the sermon, giving main points and first sub-points. Include Introduction and Conclusion.
>
> Title: Is it attractive? Clear? Honest? Related to main theme?
>
> Text: Is there a single text, or are there multiple texts? Section, chapter, paragraph, sentence phrase or word? Used literally, analogically, typologically or allegorically? Vitally related to sermon? Historical meaning accurately reflected?
>
> Central Idea: What is it? Is it formally stated? Where? Does sermon fulfill its promise?
>
> Introduction: Does it seize attention at once? Relate theme or text to hearers? Is it too long? Too short? Irrelevant?
>
> Body: Are main points clearly stated? Related to central idea? A unity? Is there forward movement? Is each point given space according to its importance? Where is climax reached?

---

[49]   O. S. Davis, *Principles of Preaching* (n.d., n.p.).

Conclusion: Does it summarize main points? Or reinforce main discussion? Or call for decision or action?

The following excerpt offers some classic feedback from the pew to the pulpit. It is entitled, *Mr. Preacher, Please!*[50] Written by James D. Furlong, it should be framed and placed on each preacher's desk in a spot where he can see it every week before he writes his weekly sermon:

> Please understand—We are hungry for a sermon that is spiritual and biblical with Christian applications rather than a lesson in social studies with metaphysical overtones;
>
> Please be at ease—We are not concerned about the degrees and titles you have won, but with the degree to which you understand human nature and its problems;
>
> Please try to avoid—The habit of scolding, moralizing and uttering endless platitudes which neither help to enlighten nor redeem our lives;
>
> Please, please speak—In your natural tone of voice—otherwise, being human, we will subconsciously tune you out and doubt your sincerity and conviction;
>
> Please do not read—From your manuscript, but look at your congregation once in a while so we can see that you believe in your heart what you are saying with your lips;

---

[50]   James D. Furlong, *Mr. Preacher, Please!*

Please omit—The classroom theological terms that are meaningless to us, but try to put the food of faith down where we may reach it and be fed;

Please be aware—That we live in a world of judgment and criticism all week long and have come to hear words of constructive appraisal and encouragement and direction, not another lecture or pious advice;

Please remember—The quality rather than the quantity and length of your sermon will help us to listen, to hear—to digest and to retain your message and thought;

Please include—A bit of relevant humor or illustration that will add seasoning and good taste to the spiritual nourishment we have come to receive at your hands;

Last and most of all, Mr. Preacher, please! Help us to see our lives with God's perspective. Help us by the insight of your words that we may gain a keener desire to do God's will—a more receptive ear to hear God's truth and greater awareness to see God's grace guiding our thoughts, giving life to our hearts and strength to our souls when we face again the changes and chances of this mortal life on Monday morning!

Humor in the Pulpit

Humor in the pulpit is like a two-edged sword. It can be cruel and destructive, but it can also be relaxing and creative. Dr. James S. Stewart, one of the greatest preachers Scotland has produced in the past forty years, has been criticized for never using humor in his sermons. He was well aware of the dangers involved.

Dr. Halford Luccock, who used humor wisely, pointed out its dangers when overused or not used properly. He said, "The man who plays constantly the role of the funny man in the pulpit is not the person to whom people will come with their troubles and sorrows. They will think, 'If I tell him, he will only make a joke of it.' "

How does one use humor wisely in the pulpit?

1. It should be kind. The brunt of the joke should be on the speaker. One of my favorites is the following. I was speaking in a city some time ago. Noticing that the collection was taken after I spoke, I asked, "What is the purpose of this collection?" The answer I received was, "To hire a better speaker next year." Or take this one. A preacher was asked, "Do you talk in your sleep?" "No," he said, "I talk in other peoples' sleep. I'm a preacher."

2. Humor is excellent for use as an attention-getter in the sermon, to wake up those who have fallen asleep, or to provide refreshing resting places. For example, if you are preaching on Father's Day, you may use this one: One Jewish father who had four married daughters said, "Three of them married doctors who can make me well for nothing, and one married a rabbi who can make me good for nothing."

3. Humor can also serve to make some unpleasant truths more palatable. For example, at the end of the sermon a woman thanked the pastor for the sermon. "I found it so helpful," she said. The preacher replied, "I hope it will not prove so helpful as the last sermon you heard me

preach." The puzzled woman asked, "Why, what do you mean?" "Well," said the pastor, "that sermon lasted you three months."

4. Humor can be used effectively to capture peoples' attention before a sermon. For example, if you are preaching on Zacchaeus, you may wish to begin with this one. A professor of homiletics had the practice of inviting one young student to the front each day, handing him a text and asking him to preach on it on the spot. One student stood up one day and said, "I have been given the name Zacchaeus. I would say, first, that he was a very little man and so am I. I would remark, secondly, that he was up a tree, and so am I. I would emphasize, thirdly, that he made haste and came down, and so will I." As the boy took his seat, the professor said to him, "Young fellow, you'll go places."

Jesus himself used humor. When he made the statement, for example, about the log in one's own eye and the speck in the neighbor's eye, he was using the humor that was in vogue in his day.

Some of the funniest humor I have heard relates to preaching. A young lady said to her pastor one day, "Your sermons are so effective. They are like water to a drowning man."

"That was a fine sermon," said the parishioner to the pastor. "Are you going to have it published?" "Only posthumously," said the pastor with a smile. "Good!" said the parishioner. "The sooner the better."

A priest was a doctor of divinity, while his wife was a doctor of medicine. Somebody called the rectory to speak to the "doctor." The housekeeper said, "Do you want the one who preaches or the one who practices?"

When used properly and naturally—avoiding sarcasm—humor can be one of the most useful and powerful tools of persuasion.

Seek a Response

A response must always be expected when the word of God is proclaimed. Indeed, we must preach for a response! When Jonah preached to the people of Nineveh, there was a response. The people believed God and repented (Jonah 3.5). When John the Baptist finished one of his sermons, the people asked him, "What then shall we do?" (Lk 3.10). When Peter finished the first Christian sermon on Pentecost, the people were so moved that they asked the apostles, "Brethren, what shall we do?" (Acts 2.37). It is still true today. When the Gospel is proclaimed, people are asking the same question silently: "What shall we do?" Most often it is the preacher who does not hear this question and does not address it.

The ultimate purpose of the sermon is to persuade, to convince the mind, to stir the will to action. If there is no response, the sermon is in vain.

Masillon, the famous French bishop, used to say, "I don't want people leaving my church saying, 'What a wonderful sermon, what a wonderful preacher.' I want them to go out saying, 'I will *do* something.' "

The sermon is not done when it is preached. It is preached; it remains yet to be done. The doing is the response we are seeking.

The Bible itself is not God's *monologue,* but rather God's dialogue with his people. Fr. George Florovsky brought this out beautifully when he wrote:

> We hear in the Bible not only the voice of God, but also the voice of man answering him—in words of prayer, thanksgiving and adoration, awe and love, sorrow and contrition, exultation, hope and despair. There are, as it were, two partners in the Covenant, God and man, and both belong together in the mystery of the true divine-human encounter, which is described and recorded in the story of the Covenant. Human response is integrated into the mystery of the word of God. It is not a divine monologue; it is rather a dialogue, and both are speaking, God and man...God wants, and expects and demands this answer and response of man. It is for this that he reveals himself to man and speaks to him. He is, as it were, waiting for man to converse with him.[51]

Part of the response to the proclamation of the Gospel is built into the Liturgy itself. Following the preaching of the sermon, which comes in the early part of the Liturgy, we are called to respond by loving one another: "Let us love one another..." Immediately following this, we are called to respond by confessing publicly our Orthodox Christian faith through the reading of the Nicene Creed. There is also the response of doxology and praise which pervades the entire Liturgy. Another response is the prayer of confession that is prayed just before Communion: "Lord, I believe and confess that you are truly the Christ..." This is the response of faith and repentance. Then comes the

---

[51]   Georges Florovsky, *Bible, Church, Tradition.*

invitation to the Last Supper and our response by coming forward to receive Christ "with the fear of God, with faith and with love." We receive him in order to respond by going out into the world to be other Christs to our fellow humans. This is the 'liturgy after the Liturgy.' Lastly, there is the response of the offertory whereby we place ourselves on the altar in complete surrender to Christ through the bread offering (*prosfora*), which represents us, and through our money offering. Then comes the specific response of the sermon we have preached: "In view of what God has done for us in Christ, dear brethren, this is what God expects as a response from us…"

Fr. Theodore Stylianopoulos has very aptly stated, "The trouble with much preaching today is that people are not, in appropriate ways, asked to respond to the good news of Christ; and if they are asked to respond at all, they are asked to do so in terms of obedience to some religious duty…when they have not yet heard the Gospel or definitely accepted its blessing."[52] First they must hear the gracious acts of God; after the hearing must come the response.

The Introduction

A man, offering a mule for sale, said to the prospective buyer, "This is a very faithful, obedient mule." Whereupon, he tried to get the mule to pull the plow to which it was hitched. But the mule stood still. It would not budge. After several unsuccessful attempts to get it started, he hit the mule over the head with a two-by-four, and the mule took off.

---

[52]   Stylianopoulos, *The Gospel of Christ*.

Said the prospective buyer to the man, "I thought you said the mule was obedient and responsive." To which the owner replied, "That he is, but you have to get his attention first."

One of the prime purposes of the introduction is to get the attention of the listener. For this reason it should be powerful. It should be able to arrest and rivet the attention of the audience to the subject about to be discussed. The introduction could be a question, a problem, a difficulty, an incident out of life, a relevant piece of humor, an illustration from literature, anything that will engage quickly the active interest and participation of the congregation.

Journalists tell us that the same is true in the newsroom. Unless the writer catches the reader's interest in the first few sentences of the story, chances are that the reader will stop reading the article and skip to another story.

A good example of the purpose of the introduction comes from the world of classical music. Many concertos begin with a crashing chord, after which they state the theme which they will develop. The reason for the crashing chord was that these concertos were originally performed in large castles or mansions. When the pianist seated himself at the piano, there was still much conversation going on. The crashing chord attracted their attention. Once this was done, the theme was stated. This is exactly the purpose served by the introduction in the sermon.

Billy Sunday, the great American revivalist preacher, was known to ride into his tent meetings on a white horse shooting two six-shooters. This was his way of riveting the attention of his listeners! This was his 'introduction.'

One clergyman began his sermon by reading a definition from the dictionary. He then asked the congregation what word he had defined. Several members called out, "Hypocrite." With that introduction he proceeded to give his homily—with everyone tuned in! He had captured their attention.

Another priest was preaching a stewardship sermon. He began this way:

> A burglar who had entered a poor priest's house at midnight tripped over a chair and woke the priest. Drawing his knife, the burglar said, 'If you yell for help, you're a dead man. I'm hunting for money.'

'Let me get up and strike a light,' said the priest, 'and I'll hunt with you.'

With his point astutely made, the priest proceeded to speak on Christian stewardship and the money the Church needed.

Another preacher began a sermon on death by telling what happened one summer morning in New York where he lived. A policeman delivered a child in a Brooklyn tenement. Less than three hours later and just a few blocks away, the same policeman shot and killed a stick-up man in self-defense. The preacher used this story of 'anonymous birth and anonymous death' to introduce his congregation to the whole mystery of life and what it's all about.

Since the purpose of the introduction is to introduce the subject, it should do just that and do it quickly. It should waste no time in getting to the main point. The danger of a long, drawn-out introduction that bores the audience and loses their attention at the very beginning is pointed out in *Mother Goose*:

> On a misty, moisty morning
> And cloudy was the weather
> And then I met an old man
> All dressed in leather.
> I began to smile
> And he began to grin
> And he said, 'How do you do?'
> And 'How do you do?'
> And 'How do you do again?'

The danger of an introduction is that there may be too much 'How do you do?' Once you have said your 'How do you do?', get straight to the point quickly. The introduction to the sermon is like the porch of a house. One doesn't linger on the porch, one crosses it quickly to get into the house wherein lies his main work.

Once a speaker loses the attention of his audience in the introduction, it will be practically impossible to regain their attention even through tactics such as shouting or pounding the pulpit. Because of the crucial importance of capturing attention, it is best not to begin the sermon with a biblical text, which can come later, but with a delightful anecdote, as Jesus did, or some arresting statement.

Attention Grabbers

We have already spoken of the necessity of capturing the attention of the listener through an arresting intro-duction. But it is not enough to capture the attention at the beginning. Once captured, the attention must be held. As one woman parishioner said to a new priest, "You're a good preacher. I enjoy you, but you don't hold me like the former priest did."

Getting the attention of a congregation is like wooing a girl. You have to keep working at it. You cannot get her attention and then forget all about her. You have to keep the listener's attention throughout the sermon. In long distance cable communication, boosters are needed every few miles to increase the signal. The same is true of a good sermon. It must have a booster every few minutes to keep it alive and vital.

Studies made in audience-listening show that serious lapses of attention occur every seven minutes. The trained public speaker will try to recapture the attention of his listeners every few minutes or so by using a graphic illustration, an anecdote, a bit of humor, a series of questions or an interesting story.

A radio personality says that he is very much aware that he can lose the attention of his audience very easily. They can turn him off with the flick of a switch. One radio announcer said once, "Oh, what a help it would be if we could only hear the click when the program is turned off!" The preacher has that advantage. He can see the 'click' if he looks for it in the faces of his hearers. They will not all be asleep, but they will have that staring kind of sleep. They will appear to be giving the speaker a very courteous kind of attention, but the mind will be wrapped in some other interest miles and miles away.

A good preacher will ever remember that he is dealing with a very brief and fragile attention span. He will respect it and work hard at keeping it.

The Conclusion

The conclusion of the sermon is so important that even if we are speaking from notes, or no notes at all, it should be written out in full and committed to memory. It not only summarizes the whole sermon, but is also the final opportunity for the preacher to drive home the point and secure a verdict from the hearers. It is here that the battle of winning a person to Christ is won or lost.

We must realize that preaching is pleading with people. It is a deliberate attempt to effect change in them. It is not a lecture. It is meant to transform as well as inform, to lead the hearer to the crisis of a spiritual decision.

The preaching of Christ is always preaching for a verdict, the verdict of commitment to the Church which is his body, his witnessing, working and worshiping community in the world for which he died.

Several years ago a prominent attorney wrote a provocative little article which was published in the *Journal of the American Bar Association*. This short essay was addressed "to the clergy." The attorney in question said that much of the failure in modern preaching could be seen easily if it were compared with the technique of attorneys in arguing cases before juries. Too often, he stated, ministers "simply announce their text, explain the circumstances surrounding it and then explain the relevant theology. At this point they have stated what we lawyers refer to as 'findings of fact' and 'conclusions of law.' " Then he went on to remark, "preachers have a way of stopping with a take-it- or-leave-it attitude."

At this point he says the lawyer "goes to work on the jury." In other words, he "pleads his case" with fervor and force and persuasiveness. If a lawyer did not do so, his client would think he had been cheated.

"Going to work on the jury" in old homiletical manuals used to be called "preaching for a verdict." We need more of this in our preaching today. We quote again these words by Dr. Harry Emerson Fosdick:

> The preacher's business is not merely to discuss repentance, but to persuade people to repent; not merely to debate the meaning and possibility of Christian faith, but to produce Christian faith in the lives of his listeners; not merely to talk about the available power of God to bring victory over trouble and temptation, but to send people out from their worship on Sunday with victory in their possession. A preacher's task is to create in his congregation the thing he is talking about.

Preaching for a verdict is what should take place in the conclusion. It is the last appeal to the jury for a decision. Or, as John Osborn put it, "If a salesman delivers an impressive sales talk, but fails to get your name on the contract, he hasn't accomplished very much. And unless the conclusion of your sermon moves your congregation to embrace the action it calls for, you haven't accomplished a great deal.... Here is where you ask your people to sign on the dotted line. Saint Paul writes to Timothy, "I charge you in the presence of God and of Christ Jesus...preach the word...convince, rebuke and exhort...." (2 Tim 4.2).

The conclusion is where you confront people with their expected response to God's word. "In view of all that has been said in this sermon, here is what God expects you to do about it."

The conclusion is not the place to tuck in a bright new thought that suddenly comes to you. This is anticlimactic and self-defeating. The place for this is in the body of the sermon. The conclusion is the gathering together of the main points of the sermon. It is pulling together all the threads. It is bringing the one big truth of the sermon into sharp focus and bearing it down in application to the hearts of the hearers so that they will understand exactly what is expected of them. It is the 'verdict' part of our preaching, an appeal to action, persuading them to do something about what they have heard. The conclusion should create the highest emotional level of the message. Instead of diminishing vocal power toward the end, the preacher should maintain full vocal power right up to the last word.

One homiletical sin congregations will not forgive is to have the preacher say, "Now in closing...," and then to ramble on for another five minutes. The purpose of a conclusion is to conclude as quickly as possible. One preacher said that in preaching he tried to do what he did on expressways and turnpikes: stay close to the right lane so he could find a good exit.

Since the sermon is conceived in prayer, written in prayer and delivered in prayer, it has always been my fervent belief that it should conclude with a prayer—a prayer that may even recapitulate reverently the main point of the sermon and the call to action.

One great American preacher, Gerald Kennedy, said, "For me the conclusion is the most difficult part of the sermon. If the conclusion is right, the most important single thing has been done."[53]

Since conclusions are so critical to the sermon, I would recommend that young preachers study the sermons of great preachers and pay special attention to the techniques used in their conclusions.

Some techniques used by preachers in the conclusion, in addition to the ones listed above, are: (1) a recapitulation of the most important points; (2) a powerful anecdote that vividly illustrates the theme and drives the point home; (3) a quotation that is pointed and strong, especially if it is the Scripture verse that has already been woven into the body of the message; (4) an appropriate question or series of questions that help the listener participate in the message; and (5) a call to action, a direct appeal to the listener to take a specific action.

I like this definition of the conclusion by John Osborn: "As the preacher moves into the conclusion, he is coming to the target. He has launched his missile; it has flown through the main divisions of his sermon. Now it is going to hit the bull's eye and bring the application home to the people."

Simplify and Clarify

When D.T. Niles, former Chairman of the Youth Department of the World Council of Churches, was in the United States many years ago, he was invited to speak at

---

[53]   *His Word Through Preaching.*

a theological school. Instead of speaking to the students he said to them, "You are learning to preach the Gospel, I want you to preach the Gospel to me. Think of me as an American pagan. I have never been to church. I have never read the Bible. The home from which I come is also pagan. I have an elementary education. I am a worker on the road." The first thing he was told by the students was, "You are a sinner." He replied, "I don't know what you are talking about. I have never heard the word 'sinner.' " The students went on preaching the Gospel to him, while he kept on saying, "I don't understand. Please use words I know." They finally ended by saying, "Such pagans don't exist."

They do exist, and unless we learn to communicate the Gospel to our listeners in words they can understand, we shall fail in fulfilling the great commission that the Lord Jesus has placed in our hands (Mt 28:19-20).

Metropolitan Chrysostomos Konstantinides of Myra, of the Ecumenical Patriarchate of Constantinople, wrote, "…the reason why Islam, popular Hinduism, modern Buddhism or other systems—largely Eastern—find a favorable reception in our strongly secularized and de-Christianized Christian areas is that these systems carry on their work among the masses in the simplest way; they present their main principles in a greatly simplified form."

Metropolitan Chrysostomos goes on to ask why the work of some conservative Protestant groups on the mission field is more effective than the same work being done by Roman Catholics who are better organized and a more unified group. He replies, "The answer is found in the general thesis stated above. The simpler and less complicated, less abstract and metaphysical a teaching is, the more positive and effective are the results. The possibility of the success of preaching that is simple and bereft of all scholasticism, of all sorts of abstract dogmatic speculation, is much greater. A complicated presentation, influenced by ideas that are foreign to the listener and overburdened with dialectical theology, is condemned to failure.

"The contemporary African or Asian has difficulty following the thought of a European theologian who loses himself in the complex and obscure ideas of a theology covered with the dust of its past...."[54]

The need for simplicity in the sermon becomes very obvious when we remember that the sermon is 'heard.' When reading a book, we can go back and reread a section that we did not first understand. In watching football games on TV, we are provided with instant replays of important episodes. When conversing with a friend, we can ask a question about a point we did not understand. But we do not provide instant replays of hard-to-understand thoughts when preaching. We do not permit questions to be asked. This makes it all the more difficult to keep up with the message being preached. If the hearer misses a sentence or two and loses the train of thought, we shall lose him.

The preacher's job is more difficult when one realizes that the television repairman can use his technical language in his repair shop. He does not have to make himself understood outside his own profession, while the preacher must make the message and language of the Gospel un-

[54]   Ion Bria (ed.), *Martyria and Mission* (Geneva, 1980).

derstandable to the television repairman, the plumber, the surgeon and the cleaning lady who sit in the congregation on Sunday.

Indeed, theology is a matter of life and death for these people. It must be communicated to them in a simple, intelligible way. Newspaper writers are told that they must write for people who have a fifth- to seventh-grade level of education. This is even more true for the preacher. In order to achieve this successfully, many great preachers have been known to test their sermons by reading them beforehand to their wives or some other lay person not trained in theology. One great preacher read his sermon to a simple, uneducated, old domestic servant, urging her to stop him every time he said something she did not understand.

It was said of one great American preacher (John H. Jowett): "Always he sought for the right word, always he labored to have the word say exactly what he wanted to say

He used short, pregnant sentences which were as clear as crystal... [He] 'wooed' words, loved them and made them blend with his experiences and thought."⁵⁵ "Speak clearly if you speak at all," said Oliver Wendell Holmes, "carve every word before you let it fall."

Frederick Meek once rephrased the words of Saint Paul as follows: "Though I speak with the tongues of men and of angels, but have not clarity, I am nothing." In writing to the Colossians, Paul speaks of the importance of clarity when he says, "Pray for us...that God may open a door

---

⁵⁵   John H. Jowett, *Great Pulpit Masters Series* (Grand Rapids, Mich., 1950).

for the word, to declare the mystery of Christ...that I may make it clear, as I ought to speak" (Col 4.2-4). How can we forget Paul's other words: "In the church I would rather speak five words with my mind, in order to instruct others, than ten thousand words in an unknown tongue." There are many today who are continuing to preach "the ten thousand words in an unknown tongue." When one parishioner asked another during the sermon, "What is he preaching about?", he received the answer, "He don't say."

When Winston Churchill turned to America for help in the Second World War, he did not say, " Supply us with the necessary inputs of relevant equipment and we shall implement the program and accomplish its objectives." No, he said very simply and plainly, "Give us the goods and we will finish the job!" In commissioning us to preach, Jesus said, "Feed my lambs" (Jn 21.15b). It was as if he said, "Put the spiritual food sufficiently low so that the little children can reach it and feed on it." It is significant—someone said—that Jesus said, "Feed my lambs"—down there. He did not say, "Feed my giraffes"—up there.

I have always been impressed with the abstract answer someone gave in answer to Jesus' question, "Who do you say that I am?" "You are the eschatological manifestation of the ground of our being, the kerygma in which we find the ultimate meaning of our interpersonal relationships." Hearing this answer, Jesus said, "What?"

I can just imagine Jesus saying the same thing about much that passes for preaching today: "What?"

If we think the above answer as to who Jesus is, is far-fetched, listen to some of the words we use in our preaching: logos, cherubim, seraphim, alpha and omega, things of the flesh, bosom of Abraham, heir of salvation, blood of the Lamb, in Christ, incarnation, atonement, repentance, etc.. When words get in the way of communication, they should either be explained simply or replaced with plainly spoken words that people can readily understand. The best homiletical gift Billy Graham has is his staccato delivery of machine-gunned sentences and his exclusive use of words everyone can understand.

Study for a moment one of the greatest, simplest and shortest speeches ever written—the Gettysburg address. There are 265 words in it. Of these, 194 are monosyllabic words! Indeed, to use the words of Walt Whitman, "Simplicity is the glory of expression."

I was impressed when I read Schopenhauer's four guidelines for writers: (1) have something to say; (2) write carefully so that everyone knows you put importance on what you have to say; (3) use clear, simple language which shows that your ideas have been thought through thoroughly; (4) remember, the simpler the expression, the deeper the impression. The ability to simplify the expression of an idea is the mark of an intelligent mind. As Augustine said, "Make the truth plain! Make the truth pleasing! Make the truth moving!" One of the best ways to achieve simplicity and clarity is to use short words, short sentences and ideas that are common to the speaker and the hearer alike, as Jesus did.

Preaching is a difficult and demanding task. More than any other public speaking exercise, a worship service brings together a broad and diverse collection of persons. Age will range from infants to octogenarians. Intellectual ability will range from retarded to genius. Social class extends from high to low; wealth, from much to none. Personal situations may include: the bored adolescent, the alcoholic presently under duress, the intellectual seeking stimulation, the anxious parent, the guilty thief, the contented family, the successful entrepreneur, those who love and those who hate the preacher, and so on.

The preacher is expected and expects to give something to all of the above. The manner of the giving is expected to be pleasant and gracious, impressive and warm, challenging and comforting, but above all, simple and clear.

We must remember that Jesus toned down his glory in order to be with us and communicate his Gospel to us. He turned on the glory at the Transfiguration and the disciples were blinded. The Transfiguration helps us appreciate the *kenosis*, the self-emptying, the degree to which Jesus stepped down in glory to be able to communicate effectively with his people using parables that everyone could understand.

Dr. Carl Sagan, scientist, scholar, author and teacher, brought the wonders of the heavens down to earth through his public television series *Cosmos* in the fall of 1980. The series attracted more viewers (as many as ten million each week) than any other regular series in Public Broadcasting Service (PBS) history. Sagan took the difficult science of astronomy, simplified and popularized it to the point where it was fun to watch. He insists, "There is nothing about science that cannot be explained to the layman."

Orthodox Christianity has a great message to bring to modern man—the message of the greatest good news this world has ever heard. But it is a message wrapped up in some difficult sounding words, words such as redemption, salvation, incarnation, sanctification, theosis, transfiguration, etc.. The message needs to be simplified and brought down to the level of the layman. It can be done. Jesus did it with theology. Dr. Carl Sagan did it with astronomy. There is nothing about theology that cannot be explained to the layman.

Clarity requires live and understandable words! Two women fish hucksters were engaged in a heated dispute in London. Their sentences were short and terse, their language direct and colorful, their delivery forceful. A professor of homiletics who happened to be present said to his student: "Stay, Sammy, stay and learn to preach!"

John of Bologna, in the year 1212, tells of how he heard Saint Francis speak. He expected great oratory from so famous a man. He found that Saint Francis spoke quietly and in the vernacular. When Francis had finished that simple sermon, however, John says, the crowd was weeping; and men, who would not scorn to shed each other's blood, turned and forgave past enmities. And as Saint Francis passed out of that place that afternoon, thousands of people knelt down to kiss the hem of his frayed brown robe as he went by. Is there any reason why a preacher of today couldn't speak that simply?

Application

G. P. Fedotov writes in *The Russian Religious Mind* concerning the state of preaching in the Byzantine Church:

> The Greek sermon was mostly theological. Its paramount aim was to disclose the meaning of a par-

ticular feast in the Church calendar and its mystical significance. The sermon itself was a continuation of the Liturgy, sharing in its solemn, theurgical style, but the moral implications were often neglected. This gives us the key to a tremendous gap in the Byzantine religion: the weakness of ethical life.[56]

It was this type of abstract theological preaching with little or no moral application to the lives of the listeners that Saint John Chrysostom tried to overcome. As Paul W. Harkins writes, "He [Chrysostom] is much more interested in instructing his people and correcting their faults; he uses his penetrating insight into the meaning of Scripture to find therein applications to the lives and conduct of his flock. And in this he is supreme."[57] The secret of Chrysostom's excellence at applying the message directly to the lives of his listeners is to be found in the fact that he applied the message of the Gospel to himself first, hoping that in this way it would speak also to the lives and needs of his hearers. As we read and pray over the Scripture on which we are to speak, it is essential that we place ourselves in the events taking place. As John Ruskin said, you "ought to imagine yourself present, as in the body, at each recorded act in the life of the Redeemer." We are there not as spectators sitting on the side and watching, but as actual participants in the events. Who is the blind man groping for the light? Myself. Who are the disciples with their stupid and misguided questions? Myself. Who are the Pharisees with their blind traditionalism? Myself. The message

---

[56]   G. P. Fedotov, *The Russian Religious Mind* (New York, 1946).

[57]   P.W. Harkins, *Ancient Christian Writers* (Westminster, MD).

must be made to apply to us first, before it can be made to apply to others. As it has been said, "Apply yourself totally to the text, and apply the text totally to yourself." The great English preacher Spurgeon said once that the sermon begins with application. Without it, a sermon is like a doctor who gives a sick man a lecture on health, but sends him out of his office without a prescription.

When we read the Epistles of Saint Paul, we see that Paul invariably gives us doctrine first and then deductions from doctrine. First, he tells us what God has done for us in Christ, and then he zeros in on our response. Because this is what God did for you, he says, this is what he now expects of you. Every doctrine is applied directly to the life of the hearer and demands a specific response of Christian living. Theology is not preached in an abstract way with no reference or application to the life of the hearer. It is very personal, direct and specific.

Often it is the application of the sermon that is abrasive to the listener. This is because it is aimed at some besetting sin. There was a preacher once who was saying to a congregation, "It is wrong to steal horses." The congregation answered, "Amen, amen." "It is wrong to steal cows." "Amen, amen." Then he said, "It is wrong to steal chickens." And someone shouted back, "Now he is meddling." The application of the sermon will often be meddlesome in the life of the listener, but that is one of the tests of its relevance.

A man was heard to say as he emerged from church, "Great sermon today! For once I felt he didn't mean me." That sermon missed its mark!

A preacher said once that people lose their souls through excessive generosity. They give the whole sermon away to others. They sit down under the sermon and when the preacher touches upon this sin or that, they don't take it to themselves, but give this part of the sermon to one brother and that part to another; soon the whole sermon is given away. Nothing is left for themselves. And we hear them say to us after the sermon, "That was a powerful sermon today, Father. Too bad so-and-so wasn't here to hear it."

It is this tendency to apply the truth we hear to everyone but ourselves that the preacher needs to overcome by emphasizing constantly that the word of God speaks 'personally' to each one of us in every sermon we hear. Every true sermon is an existential encounter between Jesus and us. Yet we cannot escape the truth that if the word of God speaks personally to the preacher, it will speak personally to those who listen. The preacher must apply the text totally to himself before he can succeed in applying it to others.

Another method that is effective for a good application is to avoid generalities and become specific. For example, when soldiers asked John the Baptist after his sermon, "And we, what shall we do?", John gave a very specific answer, zeroing in on the particular sins of a soldier: "Rob no one by violence or by false accusation, and be content with your wages" (Lk 3.14). John told them exactly what his teaching meant for them. These, then, are the marks of a good application: apply the text totally to yourself, make your hearers feel that they are not spectators but participants in the text, be personal and be specific.

The Importance of Definitions

A parish board was considering buying a chandelier for the dome of their church. They voted for it—all except the secretary. When asked why he voted against it, he said, "Well, I can give you three good reasons. In the first place, I would have to write the letter of purchase, and I don't know how to spell it; secondly, when it arrives, we have no one who can play it; and thirdly, what we really need is a light for the dome."

How much bad communication takes place because we don't know what we're talking about, we don't take the time to define the words we're using or we invest them with meaning that is simply not there?

A patient once asked his doctor, "Doctor, if there is anything wrong with me, don't frighten me half to death by giving it a long scientific name. Just tell me in plain English." "Well," the doctor replied hesitantly, "to be perfectly frank, you are just plain lazy." "Thank you, doctor," murmured the patient. "Now give me the long scientific name so I can tell my family."

Define Your Terms

One of the first principles of logic is that we begin by defining our terms. Exactly what do the words we use mean? Do they mean one thing to us and something else to the one with whom we're conversing? For, you see, we can so easily distort the meaning of words. We can make them mean what we want them to mean. We can make our own definitions to suit ourselves. A prime example of this is the Communists. They say they want peace; the Church

says it wants peace. But there is a world of difference between the 'peace' the Communists want and the peace
the Church wants. A peace that is based on tyranny is not
peace. A peace that is based on fighting God and Christ is
not peace. A peace that is based on revolution and class
warfare and brother killing brother is not peace, but the
Communists keep calling it 'peace.'

Lewis Carroll described this phenomenon a long time
ago when he put these words in the mouth of Humpty
Dumpty: "When I use a word, it means just what I choose
it to mean—neither more nor less."

So it is with the Communists. Words mean just what
they want them to mean: freedom means tyranny, peace
means war, democracy means slavery, and detente means
arming to the teeth.

Malcolm Muggeridge wrote:

> ...One of the things that appalls me and saddens me
> about the world today is the condition of words.
> Words can be polluted even more dramatically and
> drastically than rivers and land and sea. There has
> been a terrible destruction of words in our time...
> Without words we are hopeless and defenseless;
> their misuse is our undoing.[58]

Let's look at what we have done to some of the words
in our religious vocabulary since it directly affects the
preaching of God's word.

Whatever Happened to Sin?

Let's take, for example, the word 'sin.' Dr. Kark Men-
ninger, eminent psychiatrist, wrote a book a few years

---

[58]   M. Muggeridge, *The End of Christendom* (Grand Rapids, 1980).

ago entitled *Whatever Became of Sin?* His main theme is
that we have gotten smarter and have invented some new
'respectable' words for some old and ugly ways of living:
drunkards and drug addicts are called chemically depen-
dent; a prostitute is called a "call girl"; adultery is called
an "affair" and is even considered a "means to personal
fulfillment"; fornication is called "living together" or "free
love"; homosexuality is "an alternate lifestyle"; stealing is
called embezzling or "white collar crime"; murder is called
"abortion" and is even performed in hospitals, places that
are supposed to save lives; murderers are said to be tem-
porarily mentally deranged, etc.. I like these words by
John H. Jowett:

> Sin is transgression. It is the deliberate climbing of
> the fence. We see the trespass sign, and in spite of
> the warning we stride into the forbidden field. Sin
> is not ignorance; it is intention. We sin when we are
> wide awake! There are teachers abroad who would
> soften words like these. They offer us terms which
> would appear to lessen the harshness of our actions;
> they give our sin an aspect of innocence. But to alter
> the label on the bottle does not change the character
> of the contents. Poison is poison, give it what name
> we please."[59]

One of the great tricks of Satan—the great deceiver—
has always been: "Never call a sin by its right name. Call it
by a nice, fair, innocent name." We see this in the parable
of the Prodigal Son. When he left home and was wasting
his substance, he was merely "seeing the world." When he
was bankrupt through riotous living, he called it "being

---

[59]   *My Daily Meditation.*

a little wild." It was only when he landed in the barnyard with the pigs that he found the right name for his behavior. "I have sinned against heaven and before you," he said to his father. And that was the beginning of his salvation. He saw himself as he really was and called his behavior by its right name: sin.

Salvation will never come to us unless we face our sin, call it by its right name and surrender it to God. Salvation for David began when he said, "Against Thee, Thee only have I sinned, O Lord, and done that which is evil in Thy sight." He called sin by its right name.

The Word 'God'

Take another one of our sacred words, the word 'God.'

A student came to a pastor once and said, "I have decided that I cannot and do not believe in God."

"All right," said the pastor. "But describe for me the God you don't believe in."

The student proceeded to sketch his idea of God. When he finished, the pastor said, "Well, we're in the same boat. I don't believe in that kind of God either."

How many different meanings people give to the word 'God.' For many people God is one who kills babies, inflicts diseases on people and creates a place called hell for eternal punishment.

How many of us grow up with childish definitions of God that we never grow out of because we do not grow spiritually. We go through life with a kindergarten concept of God. Through our preaching we are called to pour into the word 'God' its true meaning.

What do we mean when we say 'God'? Are we talking about someone vague and abstract? Absolutely not! We mean someone very specific. We mean a real historical person, Jesus. "No one has ever seen God; the only Son, who is in the bosom of the Father, he has made him known" (Jn 1.18). Jesus, who is "in the bosom of the Father," i.e., in the closest possible relationship to him, only he can show us who the Father is. And he does! Jesus says, "He who sees me sees the Father...I and the Father are one." We look through Jesus as through a window to see God the Father. This is especially so with the Pantocrator icon of Jesus in the domes of our churches. We look through the figure of the Pantocrator Jesus to see the Father. The Father is like Jesus. Only through Jesus can we see him. Apart from Jesus, the Father remains unknown, an abstraction.

So, by 'God' we mean Jesus, but we mean more than Jesus. We mean also the Father and the Holy Spirit.

The only way we Orthodox Christians can express everything we mean by that overwhelming word 'God' is to say, "Father, Son and Holy Spirit." As Saint Theophan the Recluse said, "We are saved by the good will of the Father through the merits of the Son by the grace of the Holy Spirit."

The Word 'Happiness'

Another word that we pollute with many false meanings is the word 'happiness.' What is happiness? Happiness is not money. It is not sex. Happiness is not drugs. It is not alcohol. It is not a Caribbean cruise. It is not power or popularity. If the road to hell is paved with good intentions, the road to happiness is paved with countless false and misleading signposts or definitions.

There is only one way to happiness for the Christian, i.e., to know, love and serve the one true God. Happiness is God. Happiness is knowing that you are loved by God. As one Christian confessed, "When I look back upon the seventy years of my own life, I see quite clearly that I owe my present inner happiness, my peace, my confidence and my joy essentially to one fact: I am certain that I am infinitely loved by God." That is the true Christian definition of happiness: to live for God in Christ and to know that you are infinitely and personally loved by God and that nothing in all creation—not even death—will ever be able to separate you from the love of God in Christ Jesus. That is true happiness.

The Word 'Jesus'

Another word that needs careful definition is the name 'Jesus.

No name is more precious to Christians than the name 'Jesus!' Yet how many battles have been fought throughout history over who this Jesus was and is? Was he just man? Was he just God? Was he both God and man? Was he just the greatest teacher who ever lived? Was he just a ghost? Exactly who is this Jesus?

According to Orthodox teaching, Jesus is Lord, the eternal Son of God, the Alpha and the Omega, the Beginning and the End, the Second Person of the Holy Trinity. "He was in the beginning with God; all things were made through him, and without him was not anything made that was made. In him was life, and the life was the light of men. The light shines in the darkness, and the darkness has not overcome it" (Jn 1.2-4).

Jesus was not just God. He was not just man. He was both God and man in one and the same person, God in human flesh, God coming close to us to love us, to save us, to lift us to heaven, to make us partakers of divine nature. Truly, there is no other name under heaven given among men by which we must be saved. For "at the name of Jesus every knee bows in heaven and on earth and under the earth" (Phil 2.10).

Love

Another sacred word that has been polluted with false meanings today is the word 'love.' True love, agape, means to care deeply, to serve, to give one's life, if need be, for the one loved. The great example of this is God who "so loved the world that he gave his only Son..." Love today means anything but giving. In fact, it has come to mean not giving, but taking. Love is not agape anymore; it is lust. It is manipulating or using the other person for one's selfish gratification. It treats people as disposable pieces of Kleenex. It has done away with that deep giving of one-self called commitment in favor of just 'living together' not "until death do us part," but until some other 'meaningful relationship' comes along.

Once God is removed from life, words such as love lose their meaning completely. For how can we know what true love is without God who alone is love? Without God sacred words such as love are totally polluted and become identified with the sewer experiences of life. It is only in Christ that words—and life itself—find their true meaning.

It is the preacher's sacred task to pour into words such as love their God-given meaning.

The Word 'Sex'

Another word that has lost its meaning today is the word 'sex.' It is a word that has been taken over by the devil. It has been polluted with every kind of filth. Yet the word 'sex' does not belong to the devil. It belongs to God. He's the one who made it. After creating man and woman and ordering them to multiply, God not only said that it was "good," as he had said of all his previous creations, he now said that it was "very good" (Gen 1.31). When God created sex, he said to himself that he had created something very beautiful, very holy, truly worthy of himself. He created it for a special relationship called marriage which he blessed then as he does now. And sex, like anything else, succeeds only when you follow the manufacturer's directions.

A Symbol of Total Giving

Sexual love is a symbol. It is a sign and seal of total commitment, of the total giving of one's self to the person loved, total sharing of all that we have and are, total faithfulness and total unity. Sex is not just a physical act. It is a physical expression, but a physical expression of something that is deeply spiritual. It is an act that expresses the total giving of one's self to the one loved for all eternity. It is to love the other with all of one's mind, heart, soul and strength. It is, in fact, the most beautiful icon on earth of God's love for us. If the physical act of love does not express this total giving of one's self to the one loved, then it is a lie. It is the prostitution of something that is sacred. No relationship is ever 'meaningful' if it does not express this kind of permanent commitment and love. This is why sex outside of marriage is irresponsible and sinful according to Orthodox teaching. If the symbol of sex is cheapened through promiscuity, what symbol can a person use to express a whole, entire and permanent love? This is why promiscuity breeds the death of love and can deprive sex of meaning in one's marriage. A love that is moved and guided by the love of God ought to be—and is—the most fulfilling and meaningful love in the world. Sex can never be what it was created to be without God, never as fulfilling, never as meaningful, never as joyful, never as satisfying. That is why marriage is a sacrament in the Orthodox Church: to enhance and make possible in Christ a true and lasting sexual love that will be a symbol of total giving and a true icon on earth of God's love for man.

The task of the preacher is to reclaim the word 'sex' for God by giving it its proper definition. It needs to be cleansed and given back to God. It is his word—a sacred word for a holy love and a sacred relationship: marriage.

The Word 'Church'

Another word that needs to be defined constantly by the Orthodox preacher is the word 'church.' Look at the tremendous variety of groups that call themselves 'churches.' In fact, anyone can establish a 'church' for himself.

There are many cults and other groups today that use the name 'Jesus' and 'church' very freely. You'll hear them calling themselves 'Jesus People' or Jesus Church.' But are they truly churches? Were they founded by Jesus and the apostles? What kind of historical connection do they have with the apostles and the Early Church? If they devil appears as an angel and quotes Scripture, then he can use even 'churches' to lead people away from the one true God and his plan of salvation.

We need to define our terms carefully. Exactly what do we mean when we say 'church?' We Orthodox Christians mean by 'Church' the body through which Christ is present and active in the world today. It was founded by Christ through the apostles and has maintained a living, historical connection with the apostles through the ordination of its clergy. The fact that the bishop who ordained me can trace his ordination historically all the way back to the apostles and through them to Christ is a guarantee that the Orthodox Church was not founded by someone called Joe Smith a few centuries ago, but by Christ himself, and that it traces its existence historically back to Jesus. We call this apostolic succession. It is the authentic and genuine Church or body of Christ in the world today. It continues to teach not one man's interpretation of the faith, but the complete deposit of faith as it was handed down to the apostles by Jesus.

So there are some very important questions to ask when one hears the word 'church.' Was this church founded by God or by man? Does it have an unbroken historical connection with the early Apostolic Church? How else can I be certain that what it teaches is truly apostolic, truly Christian, truly the word of God and not one man's interpretation or misinterpretation of that faith?

A church is the true Church of Christ if it can show historically that it was founded by Christ and has maintained a living connection over the centuries with that Early

Church. We need this historical connection in order to be assured that the deposit of the faith has not been tampered with, but has been handed down to us in its entirety.

Conclusion

How easily we can be misled if we do not pause to define some of the words we use—words that can so easily lose their true meaning in today's world, i.e., words such as sin, God, happiness, sex, Jesus, love, church and so many more. For the devil delights in polluting words. He never calls a thing by its right name, but by something that sounds very innocent.

The preacher's task is to define words very carefully. If he is preaching on joy, he must define joy as carefully as possible. The great American preacher Harry Emerson Fosdick wrote,

> When a preacher deals with joy, let us say, he ought to start, not with joy in the fifth century B.C., nor with joy as a subject to be lectured on, but with the concrete difficulties in living joyfully that his people actually experience. He should have in mind from the start their mistaken ideas of joy, their false attempts to get it, the causes of their joylessness, and their general problem of victorious and happy living in the face of life's puzzling and sometimes terrifying experiences. This is a real problem for everybody, and the sermon that throws light on it is a real sermon.[60]

---

[60] Harry Emerson Fosdick, "What is the Matter with Preaching?" *Harper's Magazine* (1928).

5
Delivering the Sermon

The preacher will be aided in the delivery of the sermon by developing and maintaining the proper mood in the congregation before the sermon is delivered. This mood has already been established by the Liturgy. It is one of prayer, worship and receptivity to the word of God. One of the worst things we can do in the delivery of the sermon is to destroy this worshipful mood by preceding the sermon with announcements about bazaars, festivals, dances, etc., all of which can be mimeographed in a bulletin and placed in the hands of the parishioners as they enter church. I cannot emphasize sufficiently the importance of maintaining the mood of worship already created by the Liturgy as the proper setting in which the word of God is to be preached. To destroy this mood through the introduction of extraneous material immediately before the sermon is to distract the attention of the listeners from the holy and to lose their attention.

The Actual Delivery

A young pastor, who had for the first time heard his sermon played back to him on a tape, said, "We've got a disaster on our hands. I've never heard a more monotonous speech. It was the same pace, no increase in pace or decrease for emphasis, very little fluctuation. I didn't know this was the way I sound. How could people bear to listen to me?"

Many preachers use a very artificial tone in preaching. How can they be made to discover the difference? Here is one way. If they will remain at the pulpit for questions after the sermon, it will be noticed that the tone of voice used in answering questions is markedly different from that used in preaching. There is a sudden shift from a formal, if not artificial, preaching style into natural, direct communication.

It seems that our concept of preaching God's word is so exalted, and our image of ourselves so low, that we feel we must assume an unnatural tone in delivering God's word. While it is true that no one is adequate to this exalted task, it certainly does not call for pretense and a phony pulpit 'performance.' God wishes to use us as we are with the gifts he has given us. He wants us to give him a chance to use us by being ourselves, not by pretending to be other than we are.

Warren W. Wiersbe writes:

> God has put variety into the universe, and he has put variety in the Church. If your personality doesn't shine through your preaching, you're only a robot. You could be replaced by a cassette player and per-

haps nobody would know the difference. Do not confuse the art and the science of preaching. Homiletics is the science of preaching, and it has basic laws and principles that every preacher ought to study and practice. Once you've learned how to obey these principles, then you can adapt to them, modify them and tailor them to your own personality.[61]

You are not called to preach like someone else. You are unique. You are called to know yourself, be yourself, accept yourself and develop your best self if your preaching is to be effective.

It is essential that you be natural in the pulpit. Be your real self, the person people see the rest of the week. Nobody likes phonies, especially in the pulpit. Do not present God's truth as if it were fiction. Few things turn people off more than a 'stained glass' voice. Another good test to apply to see if you have this sanctimonious 'stained glass' voice is to stop in the middle of the sermon and in the same tone of voice to ask the usher to close the window. If you sound ridiculous, you have a bad case of an unnatural, artificial, affected and phony 'stained glass' voice.

It is significant that the word 'homily,' often used for preaching, is derived from the Greek word *homilo*, which means 'to speak in a conversational way,' as distinguished from the affected manner of the classical Greek orator. We find the word *homilo* in the New Testament (Lk 24.14, Acts 24.26, Acts 20.11). In each instance it is used to express the thought of one person speaking to another about some-

---

[61]   Warren W. Wiersbe, "Your Preaching Is Unique," *Leadership 2*, no. 3 (1981).

thing that really matters, rather than like a lecture being delivered by a professor before a class.

To achieve the conversational tone in preaching it is important to remember that even if there are 5,000 people listening to you, there is really only one person out there listening to you. No one hears you as a crowd. Everyone hears you as an individual. You are talking to one person. So be natural. Be yourself.

One night as the great preacher Dwight L. Moody was walking to his home, he overheard two people talking. One asked, "Did Moody preach tonight?" The other replied, "No, he didn't preach. He only talked!"

Later Moody commented, "If I can only get people to think I am talking with them and not preaching at them, it is a dead easy way to get their attention."

One who knew Moody well said of his preaching, "It was straight talking, lit with illustrations always to the point and backed by his great skill in dealing with the personal problems of individuals."

Speaking on the importance of the delivery in the overall effectiveness of the sermon, Charles Reynolds Brown, one of the Lyman Beecher lecturers on preaching, said:

> Here is the final test! Here you win or lose!...the proof of the pudding is in the eating. Here in the delivery of your sermon the nourishment which you have brought for a hungry congregation is either eaten with relish, satisfaction and resultant strength, or it is left on the plate as a bit of cold victuals, useless and repellent. Take heed, therefore, how you deliver!...Many sermons are not 'delivered' at all. The minister gets his words out; he gets the sermon off

his mind and out of his system, but he does not lodge it in the minds and hearts of the people to whom it is addressed.[62]

Of course, what precedes the delivery, i.e., the content of the sermon, is also important. I recall the story of a preacher who was weak in content, but powerful in delivery. The church sexton found his manuscript in the pulpit on Monday morning. In the margin he noticed instructions in red ink saying, "Pause here," "Wipe brow here," "Look up here." At the end of the manuscript was a paragraph opposite which were written in capital letters the words, "ARGUMENT WEAK HERE. YELL LIKE H...!" Important as it is, delivery can never be a substitute for a well-prayed and well-reasoned content that speaks potently to the real needs of people.

It is important to remember that both the eye and the ear are involved in preaching. The communication taking place is both verbal and non-verbal. Studies have shown that, of the two, the non-verbal is more effective in communicating a message. According to one study, seven percent of a message comes through words, thirty-eight percent through tone of voice and fifty-five percent through body language. In another study, eighty-five percent comes to us through our eyes, eleven percent through our ears and four percent through our other senses. In other words, more than half the message is gained not from words, but from body language which includes all physical movements: the eyes, the face, the posture, the hands, etc.. It is possible, for example, for the preacher to be saying

---

[62]   Charles R. Brown, *The Art of Preaching* (New York, 1922).

one thing with his mouth and the opposite thing with his body language. By so doing he is, in effect, canceling out his message. It was said of one great preacher that when he preached, the whole man preached—his voice, his hands, his lips, his face, his gestures, his life, his whole being!

One of the most important aspects of non-verbal communication, or body language communication, in preaching is eye contact. The sermon must be so mastered that the eyes are left free to communicate with the eyes of the listeners. Eye-to- eye contact says that God is speaking to you just as though no other person were present; it is like a laser beam of communication between pulpit and pew. Eye contact gives the preacher immediate feedback. He sees whether his people are bored or interested, restless or caught up in the subject. When a congregation hears a preacher who is not looking at them, they get the impression that the message is not for them. Look at a person eyeball to eyeball and you are saying: "I mean you. I am talking to you!"

In preaching, then, the priest must look directly into the faces of his congregation in an eyeball-to-eyeball confrontation. He must preach with the skill of a violinist playing a concerto, changing his tempo, varying his voice, sinking at times to a whisper, pausing and rising to controlled crescendos. He will shift gears often, going from the 'fact' gear to the 'emotional' gear, to the 'affirmative' gear.

Good delivery is not something that happens overnight. It is something that we must work many years to develop. In his beginning years the famous actor Clark Gable had an extremely bad pitch of voice when he spoke. His wife, a trained speech expert, had to work with him for a period of many years before he could overcome this serious impediment. But he did and went on to become a truly great actor. A good style of delivery is something we must strive to develop.

Nothing, however, can affect our style of delivery as much as prayer and a personal knowledge of our Savior Jesus. The following story illustrates this point.

Some years ago at a drawing-room function, one of England's leading actors was asked to recite for the pleasure of his fellow guests. He asked if there was anything special that his audience would like to hear. An aged minister arose and said, "Could you, sir, recite the Twenty-Third Psalm?"

A strange look passed over the great actor's face. He paused for a moment and then said, "I can, and I will upon one condition, and that is that after I have recited it, you, my friend, will do the same." Impressively, the great actor began the psalm. His voice and his intonation were perfect. He held his audience spellbound; and as he finished, a great burst of applause broke from the guests.

Then, as it died away, the aged minister arose and began to recite. His voice was not remarkable; his intonation was not faultless. When finished, no sound of applause broke the silence, but there was not a dry eye in the room; and many heads and hearts were bowed in reverent awe!

The great actor rose, laid his hand upon the shoulder of the aged minister and said to the audience, "I have reached your eyes and ears, my friends. This man has reached your hearts. The difference is just this: I know the Twenty-Third Psalm, but he knows the Shepherd."

To truly know the Shepherd will make the greatest difference in the style of our delivery. It will produce a style that is honest, sincere, unaffected, warm, loving, caring, personal, convincing, uplifting and life-changing.

Preach with Love

It is important that the sermon be preached with love. Goethe once said that we learn only from those who love us. The voice with which we deliver the sermon must radiate love. It should be gentle and warm, not critical or scolding. Most of us are very sensitive to a person's voice. Instantly we can tell whether a person is sincere or not, whether the words are true or false, whether he truly loves us or not.

Love will persuade people to do what the preacher wishes them to do much more than superior knowledge or first-rate delivery of a sermon. A young man went to a great preacher one day and said, "I love to preach, but nothing happens when I preach." The famous preacher turned to the young man and said, "But, young man, do you love people?"

Beginning with Jesus, who loved us to the cross, and Saint Paul, who was willing himself to be "accursed and cut off from Christ" for the sake of his brethren (Rom 9.3), all great preachers were possessed of true love for God's people. One famous preacher said to his people, "Believe me, I am willing to go to prison and death for you, but I am not willing to go to heaven without you." If a preacher has built a bridge of love to his parishioners, his sermons will be preached to receptive minds and hearts. It was Alexander Whyte who wrote this beautiful postscript which deserves to be in every pastor's study:

> Truth often separates:
> Love always unites.
> 'Love me,' says Augustine, 'and then say
> anything to me and about me you like.'

Better than putting "the fear of the Lord" into people is to instill in them the love of Jesus. It is vain to preach any sermons at all unless, as Saint Paul says, the one who preaches has love in his heart both for God and for God's people. "Give them hell," someone said to a preacher. "No," he replied, "they have enough of hell. I'll give them heaven." Without love we are indeed "a noisy gong or a clanging cymbal" (1 Cor 13.1). The preacher may be a good student, a capable administrator, an inspiring liturgist, but above all, beyond all and within all, he must be absorbed by a total love for the people to whom he is called to minister. This is the supreme qualification of the effective preacher.

I repeat the communication statistics which tell us that in trying to get our point across in communicating with people, only seven percent of what's heard depends on the actual words we use. A full thirty-eight percent of what gets our point across is based on the way we say what we say, the inflection of our voice or the expressions we use. But fifty-five percent of our effectiveness in communicating depends on whether the person trusts us or not.

It's the same in communicating and reaching others for Christ. It isn't enough to use the right words. It's important that we use the right words with the right tone of voice—speaking the truth in love! A church marquee said it like this: "People don't care how much you know until they know how much you care!"

When you communicate your love for others not only with words but also with actions, you speak a language they can understand. You're speaking the language that Jesus spoke—a language of love.

A former communist who returned to Christianity wrote a book about some of the things that the communists did from which he felt Christians could learn something. One of the things he mentioned was that communists were told to go into a factory or plant and for six months to say nothing about communism, but concentrate on earning the respect of their fellow workers. They were to earn the right to be heard. After a time, they were free to share a little communist thought. But by then they had a platform from which to speak. They had credibility in the eyes of the workers. They had earned the right to speak. So it is that the preacher must earn the right to speak by listening to his people and by loving them.

A marvelous little story illustrates the importance of preaching God's word with love. A church member and a visitor were discussing the new pastor just after his first sermon. "Why did you ask the other preacher to resign?" the visitor asked. "Because," said the member, "He always preached that if we didn't mend our ways we would all go to hell." "But," said the visitor, "that is just what this preacher said today." "I know," was the reply, "but the other preacher acted as if he were glad of it."

Even if the sermon being preached is on hell, it will not be resented if it is preached with love. "Now abide faith, hope and love, these three; but the greatest of these is love" (1 Cor 13.13).

Preach with Enthusiasm

The speaker was dull
And his tongue seemed to trip.
He gave an address But it had no ZIP.

The Christian preacher is a herald (*keryx*) who brings the greatest good news this world has ever heard. Our Lord expects him to tell it enthusiastically. Imagine with what enthusiasm one would announce the good news of a just discovered cure for cancer. God has entrusted us with announcing the cure for a greater evil than cancer, i.e., the cure for sin, evil and death. We who proclaim it are to be aglow and tingling with a mighty excitement, an excitement that is one kindled heart setting others aflame. "We are to philosophize (theologize)," said Saint Gregory of Constantinople, "not in an Aristotelian manner (*aristotelikos*), intellectually, but in the manner of a fisherman (*alieutikos*) who is determined to catch fish." We are to preach with enthusiasm.

Where does this enthusiasm come from? Jesus said, "I came to cast fire upon the earth, and would that it were already kindled" (Lk 12.49). What is this fire? The burning bush, where Moses heard God speak and felt his presence, is no more. It has been replaced with a heart that is aflame with the presence of God. The "burning bushes" that God has in the world today are the hearts of his Pentecost people turned on by faith and fueled by the Holy Spirit. "The spirit of man is the candle of the Lord," we read in Scripture (Prov 20.27). When the fire of the Holy Spirit burns our hearts, it is all that fire is and does all that fire does. It sets us aflame with enthusiasm for God. It sets our tongues aflame with fire when we preach God's word. As we read of the early apostles, "Tongues of fire appeared which parted and came to rest on each of them. All were filled with the Holy Spirit" (Acts 2.3).

Saint Symeon the New Theologian says that our soul is like a votive lamp. In order to burn, it must have oil or wax. It must also have a good wick. These he compares to the virtues which must adorn the life of a Christian. But, above all, he says the lamp must receive fire from somewhere. It must be illuminated. The fire, he says, is the Holy Spirit which descended on the apostles at Pentecost in tongues of fire. "God is fire," he says, "and through the Holy Spirit God searches for material to set on fire with divine love."

After the apostles were baptized "with the Holy Spirit and with fire" on Pentecost, they went about lighting fires in others. They did nothing coldly. They were passionate in their love for Jesus. When they spoke of Jesus, others were kindled by their zeal. Fire kindled fire.

An English bishop visited a priest in his diocese. He asked him how his parish was doing. "Well, I can't put the Thames River on fire!" replied the priest. "What I want to know," shot back the bishop, "is if we take you out and drop you into it, will it sizzle? Are you on fire?" Father John of Kronstadt said once, "Your Lord is fire; do not let your heart be cold, but burn with faith and love."

In order to preach God's word with fire and enthusiasm it is necessary to guard the life of the Spirit within us, to keep the inner flame burning. If pastors suffer from what is so appropriately called 'burn-out,' it is because the fire of God's Spirit within has been allowed to burn out. No tongue can ever speak with fire if the flame of God's Spirit in the preacher's heart is quenched.

A layman once took his priest to a football game. During the game the layman turned to his priest and said, "Father, look how those young men on the field are playing. They're giving all they've got with enthusiasm. Why don't you preach that way?" The priest thought for a moment and then replied, "I would if I had all those people cheering for me."

What that priest forgot was that every time he preaches he has the greatest cheering section in the world, i.e., the Father, the Son, the Holy Spirit, Saint Peter, Saint Paul, Saint John and all the other saints in heaven are cheering and praying for him! This should really set him on fire!

Leon Trotsky, the early communist leader, was one of the world's greatest orators. It is said of him: "His animal energy, his gift for couching generalizations in simple, emotional terms made him an ideal mass speaker." A friend said that he had seen and heard Trotsky speak for two and a half to three hours to a completely enthralled audience which was not seated, but had to stand all the time. His oratory was a combination of lyricism, emotion and logic powered by his passionate theatricality. His wife said of him, "He spoke with his whole being; it seemed as though with every such speech he lost a little of his strength—he spoke to them with so much blood."

Trotsky was filled with an unholy spirit. The Christian preacher is filled with the Holy Spirit. Tell me, who should be the better speaker?

The King Is in the Audience

A play in England was suddenly interrupted by the playing of the national anthem. In the wings the stage manager and director ran from actor to actor whispering excitedly, "Give it all you've got tonight! Play as you've never played before." "Why?" they asked. "Because," came the quick reply, "King George has just come in. The king is in the audience!"

The Christian preacher should ever remember that the King is always in the audience. He should give the sermon all he's got and preach as he has never preached before.

It was a vision of the presence of the King in the audience that inspired Chrysostom to become a great preacher. According to legend, he saw a vision where he was in the pulpit, and in the altar area and round about him were holy angels. In the midst of them and directly before him was the Lord Jesus; and he was to preach to the congregation assembled beyond. From that moment on, Chrysostom never forgot that vision. Whenever he mounted the pulpit to preach, it was always with this vision in mind.

Longinos, the great Greek literary critic, offered his students the following test for good writing and good speaking:

"When you write anything, ask yourself how Homer or Demosthenes would have written it; and, still more, ask yourself how Homer and Demosthenes would have listened to it."

This is also a good test for the Christian preacher. When we speak for Christ, we must speak as if Christ were listening. He is—so are all the saints in heaven. We could not possibly have a better cheering section!

Be Not Discouraged

One of the most discouraging elements in preaching is the fact that we see no immediate results. Here we need to be reminded that it is our job only to sow and to keep sowing. The one who gives growth to the seed is God. If we will sow faithfully, God will give the growth according to his time schedule, not ours. It is our business to sow seed. It is God's business to give the 'increase.' He knows the right time and place to bring the seed to fruition. We must not jump to the conclusion that nothing has been accomplished just because we see no immediate visible results. The work may have already begun which will manifest itself later on. We must pray constantly that God will prepare the soil into which we shall sow the seed, making it receptive, and that he will give growth to the seed once it is sowed. Important as the preacher's task is, so much depends on God! "I planted, Apollos watered, but God gave the increase. So neither he who plants, nor he who waters, is anything, but only God who gives the growth.... For we are fellow workers for God; you are God's field, God's building" (1 Cor 3.6-9).

"Do you expect to make an impression on the heathen?" a missionary was asked. His answer was, "No, but I expect God will."

Sermons That Started Something

Even though we do not always see immediate results after a sermon is preached, it is important to remember that some great projects in life were started by sermons. Many great schools and universities—among them Northwestern, Princeton, Harvard—and many hospitals were inspired by sermons.

Dr. Crawford Long of Jefferson, Georgia, who was the first to develop anesthetics, said that he got his idea from the text of a sermon in church: "The Lord caused a deep sleep to fall on Adam." It was a sermon that stopped the war between Chile and Argentina which ended with both nations erecting the beautiful statue of Christ on the mountain, the Christ of the Andes. It was a forceful sermon, preached after Aaron Burr shot Alexander Hamilton in a duel, that set in motion the initial law that eventually put an end to dueling in America. It was through the preaching of Saint Ambrose that Augustine was converted. It was because of the inspirational influence of a sermon that the National Safety Council was established in New York in 1911. It was at a communion service that Harriet Beecher Stowe, in a flash of insight, got her idea for Uncle Tom's Cabin, which played such an important role in the outlawing of slavery. Following the sermon, she went straight to her bedroom with tears in her eyes, walking as though in a trance. Then she set down on paper the outline of the vision she has seen before God's altar. A great contemporary psychiatrist, Dr. Karl Meninger, wrote concerning the importance of preaching:

The minister, standing before his flock week after week, speaking to them for half an hour under aesthetic and hallowed auspices, has an unparalleled opportunity to lighten burdens, interrupt and redirect circular thinking, relieve the pressure of guilt feelings and their self-punishment and inspire individual and social improvement. No psychiatrists or psychotherapists, even those with many patients, have the quantitative opportunity to cure souls and mend bodies which the preacher enjoys.[63]

The Preacher's Health

We have said much about the care and feeding of the preacher's spiritual life, yet just as important is the concern for the preacher's physical life. A cardiologist said once that his practice was made up mostly of clergy and his own fellow physicians. Both professions are called to share so much of other people's problems that an enormous amount of strength goes out of them. They are so busy that they cannot find time for relaxation. The results of the emotional strain become all too visible in the breakdown of the physical organism. No one was busier than Jesus, yet he deliberately set time aside to go apart and be in a quiet place.

In order to function as an effective preacher of God's word, the preacher must realize the importance of a sound mind and a sound soul in a sound body. There should be ample sleep, a regular program of daily exercise, at least one day off each week, indoor and outdoor games with his children and others, and a restful vacation each year. We

---

[63]   Karl Meninger, *Whatever Became of Sin?* (New York, 1973).

have this great treasure in an earthen vessel, but let's try to keep this vessel as healthy as possible.

Conclusion

Speaking of the preachers of God's word, Father Karl Rahner says:

> They speak a human word. But it is filled with divine truth...they go and deliver the message. And the miracle happens: they actually find men who hear the word of God in this odd talk, men into whose heart the word penetrates, judging, redeeming and making happy, consoling and dispensing strength in weakness, even though they say it, even though they deliver the message badly. But God is with them, with them in spite of their misery and sinfulness. They preach not themselves, but Jesus Christ; they preach in his name. To the marrow of their bones they are ashamed that he said, Whoever hears you, hears me; whoever despises you, despises me.' But he said it. And so they go and deliver the message. They know that it is possible to be sounding brass and tinkling cymbal and to be oneself lost after having preached to others. But they have not chosen themselves. They were called and sent. And so they have to go and preach. In season and out, they traverse the fields of the world and scatter the seed of God. They are thankful when a little of it grows. And they implore the mercy of God for themselves so that not too much of it remains unfruitful through their fault. They sow in tears. And usually it is someone else who reaps what they have sowed. But they know this: the word of God must run and bring fruit;

for it is God's blessed truth... (bringing) comfort in
death, and hope of eternal life.[64]

What better way to conclude these thoughts on preaching than with the following words of Saint Basil from his
Moral Rule 80 in which he describes the qualities and
functions of those who are called to preach God's word:

> What manner of men does Scripture wish those to
> be who are entrusted with the proclamation of the
> Gospel? As apostles and ministers of Christ and
> faithful stewards of God's mysteries, fulfilling only
> the things commanded by the Lord without falling
> short in deeds or words; as heralds of the kingdom
> of heaven, for the destruction of him who holds the
> power of death in sin; as a type or rule of piety, to
> establish the complete rectitude of those that follow
> the Lord, and to rebuke the perversity of those who
> in any way whatsoever disobey Him; as an eye in a
> body, since they discern between good and evil and
> guide the members of Christ towards what benefits
> each; as shepherds of the sheep of Christ, not even
> shrinking from laying down their lives for their sakes
> on occasion, that they may impart them the Gospel
> of God; as doctors, with much compassion by their
> knowledge of the teaching of the Lord healing the
> diseases of souls, to win for them health in Christ
> and perseverance; as fathers and nurses of their
> own children, in the great affection of their love in
> Christ willing to render to them not only the Gospel
> of God, but even their own souls; as God's fellow
> workers, having given themselves wholly on behalf

---

[64]   Karl Rahner, *Meditations on the Sacraments* (New York, 1977).

of the Church to such works only as are worthy of God; as planters of God's branches, inserting nothing that is alien to the vine which is Christ, or that fails to bear fruit, but improving with all diligence such as belong to Him and are fruitful; as builders of God's temple, shaping the soul of each one so he fits harmoniously on to the foundation of the apostles and prophets.[65]

---

[65]   Fedwick, *Basil.*

CPSIA information can be obtained
at www.ICGtesting.com
Printed in the USA
FFHW022222191119
56094158-62152FF